DEMON SEER

THE AWAKENING

Written By

June Lundgren

DARKNESS CANNOT EXTINGUISH THE LIGHT.
THE LIGHT WILL PREVAIL NO MATTER HOW DARK.
A TINY FLICKER OF LIGHT CAN PIERCE THE DARKEST NIGHT.

PROLOGUE

People ask what a Demon Seer is. A demon seer is a person in which an archangel soul resides. Which allows the person to see, hear, understand and remove negative entities from the physical world. In extreme cases, the angelic soul can kill the negative entity.

CHAPTERS

What to Expect	6
Man and the Darkness	11
God Hears Us	17
Negative Awareness	23
Tools for Communication	27
Negative Influence	31
Demon Thinking	39
How Demons Work	44
Hierarchy	50
Evolution of Angels and Demons	54
Inside Information	56
The Soul	60
What Not to Do	69
Doorways Into Our World	73
How Demons Move Through Our World	76
Demons Are Everywhere	79
Old Demons	82
Perception	105
Spirit Attachments	108
Possession	112

Protection	132
Death the Final Exit Point	148
Angelic Connection	158
Shadow People	161
War Between Heaven and Hell	164
Spiritual Warfare	166
Lucifer	170
Haunted Objects	174
Grim Reaper	178
Hearing the Other Side	189
Through My Eyes	195
Help From Above	199
Curses	208
How to Help Yourself and Where to Find Help	211
Glossary of Common Terms	219

WHAT TO EXPECT

I am putting pen to paper to help people understand that negative entities exist and walk among us daily. The purpose of this book is to bring awareness to the world.

It seems to be the consensus that you must be a bad person to have a negative entity single you out and attach itself to you; nothing could be further from the truth. If the person is already 'bad,' what is the attraction? It gains the negative entities nothing. However, if they attach themselves to a person of faith, then they have the chance to turn that person away from the light or make them doubt their faith in God. I have seen devout Christians end up with some of the worst attachments. Negatives have ways to infiltrate a person's life without the person becoming aware of it until it's too late. They can change and influence the choices we make in our daily life.

This book will help to open the world's eyes to the darkness that moves among us in the physical world. People need to recognize the presence of evil and where to find help when it is needed. I hear from people almost daily about how they have suffered from a negative entity attachment or influence for weeks, months, and even years.

Unfortunately, people have little to no resources to help them in this situation. When the person encounters a negative entity, they are afraid their friends will think they are crazy or trying to get attention. Even their own family do not always believe what is happening until they experience the activity. People fail to realize that if you have a demonic attachment, it doesn't just affect you; it affects anyone close to you. Everyone is a target, and everyone is in danger.

This book will answer many questions, such as:

- What do demons want from the living?
- Why and how are negative entities attracted to an individual or a location?
- What will ward off these beings?
- How can you protect yourself?
- What is a negative entity?
- Where did negative entities originate?
- How can you distinguish between a negative earthbound spirit and a demon?
- How do you know if you've had an encounter with one of them?
- What do you do if you do encounter one of them?
- How do you know if you have one attached to you or in your home?
- What are the signs and symptoms?
- Why me? What attracted the entity to me?

- How can we fight what we can't see?
- Where can I go to get help?

I will help you understand how negative beings see the living. What their intent is regarding the living. How the negative entities evolved into what they are and what purpose they serve. Is God aware of this issue, and what is He doing to help the living?

I answer these questions and many more in this book.

Webster's dictionary defines a demon as an evil spirit or devil; especially one thought to possess a person or act as a tormentor in hell.

I define a demon as a negative spiritual being that cannot be reborn into a physical body. It seeks only to bring as much pain and suffering to humans as possible. One of the reasons for this is each physical body contains a white light soul. These souls are the ones who helped to defeat the dark ones and send the negatives into the dark realm. I have been fighting these beings for more than forty years and winning the battles in hopes of winning the war.

There are angels and demons in the world today, fighting a battle for the souls of all senescent beings. It may sound dramatic, but it's true; spiritual warriors are growing in numbers daily.

These spiritual warriors are everyday people called to fight against the darkness, infiltrating the world over the centuries.

Once the Great War between Lucifer and his followers ended, God created a rift into a darker dimension. The fallen angels were forced into the rift to live in darkness for the rest of their existence. Over time they have grown bitter and vengeful. Eventually, they figured out a way to enter our world and influence people, and ruin lives.

Although demons are negative, a tiny part of them remains a part of the light. It is buried deep within them. Occasionally something will spark the light deep within them, and just for a moment, they remember what it was like to live in the light. This spark of light quickly quelled and soon forgotten, but occasionally, a long-forgotten spark ignites. Unable to dispel the spark of light, the dark entity may ask to return to the light. If they are sincere in their need to return home, God grants them their request.

Negative entities move stealthily behind the scenes and in the shadows. They will whisper in people's ears and put thoughts into their heads to influence them. They may make suggestions that will impact a person's life or the lives of those around them. Ultimately their goal is to make the person's life a living hell.

But God has been watching the movements and actions of the negatives. Unbeknownst to the dark realm, he has been sending help into the world through angelic warriors reborn into physical bodies. He has sent eight archangels to be born into physical bodies to do his work. These archangels are demon slayers and assassins.

MAN AND THE DARKNESS

Man has always been fascinated with the forbidden. Since the beginning of creation, we have always pushed the envelope as far as possible. People seem to think they can play with the dark ones and never pay the price.

Why you may ask yourself, why would anyone want anything to do with dark entities? Some people worship the dark ones and try to conjure them. These people do rituals designed to open doorways into our world. They do this to bring these entities into our world and serve them. They fail to understand that these creatures serve no one but themselves. It is too late when the person who conjured them realizes they have no control over the entity.

Here are some of the reasons people choose to engage with these beings.

- It's a challenge.
- To prove they can do it.
- We are seeking a thrill.
- To rail against society.
- They are seeking acceptance.
- Power and wealth.

There is always a price to pay for dealing with dark ones, no matter the reason. The price may not be visible initially but soon becomes glaringly apparent. The person's mental, emotional, and physical health declines rapidly. Even with everything they are experiencing, the person blames their 'bad luck' on everything else. They are loathed to admit that their dabbling in the dark arts sent their lives spiraling downwards.

Now, as never before in man's history, people are seeking answers to what lies beyond our world. Paranormal ghost hunting shows have become the norm, whereas they were the exception twenty years ago. People are not tuning in to these shows for educational purposes. They are tuning in to these shows to glimpse a ghost or demon. They expect to see the people investigating interact with ghosts or demons. They will watch movies, such as poltergeist, Insidious, or the Ring, and believe what happens on the screen is true and accurate. After watching many of these shows, the person suddenly becomes an expert on the paranormal.

They believe that they know better than the other people who have been doing it for years. They have the attitude that they are impervious to anything they may encounter. They create a team and go out to investigate local hauntings in the hope of catching something on film that has never been caught before. Their ultimate goal is to get their paranormal television show. These people have no idea what they are up against. They are hopelessly out of their element and unprepared for encountering even the simplest of entities, let alone something negative.

There was a time when people were God-fearing, and it kept them on the straight and narrow. Nowadays, many people have no regard for the spiritual side of life. They do what they like without regard to anyone else, including God.

People have become more self-involved and less likely to help their fellow man. We have become disillusioned with religion because many televangelists seek monetary gain and scandalous Catholic Church accusations. Many people are turning to science or, worse, the dark arts. Instead of seeking the answers from within themselves, they seek acceptance from those connected with negativity and darkness. It's kind of like a teenager joining a gang to gain acceptance.

Every religion out there has the same problem with increased negative activity. The churches don't want people to know that encounters with Inhumans are on the rise. Even the Vatican itself has admitted to an overwhelming number of possessions occurring worldwide.

Humans believe we are in control of our lives, but control is an illusion. Encountering a ghost, let alone a dark entity is the farthest thing from most people's minds.

The dark ones are waiting and watching, always lurking behind the scenes watching for an opportunity to cause the ruination of a person's life and those whom they love. They are more prevalent than humanity is aware of, and they infiltrate every fiber of man's world, just waiting for the perfect moment to cause pain and destruction.

Considering how easily influenced and self-absorbed people have become, it's not all that hard. Man has become pretty good at screwing up their lives and the lives of others without even trying. When things go wrong, we always blame God, accusing him of punishing us. When in reality, He doesn't have to do anything, we can screw up our lives all by ourselves.

But the negatives want to make certain we do it right, so they whisper in our ears and give us a push in the wrong direction. Sometimes they take over our lives, completely adding pain, suffering, and chaos to the mix.

People are under the misconception that they would know if they had an attachment. It is not always the case; you may have unknowingly had a negative entity observing you for weeks, months, or even years. They will not show themselves until they have watched the person for some time and have learned all their weaknesses, strengths, and desires. They peer into the person's mind to see if their faith is strong or weak and who or what is important to them. Then they figure out how they can use it against them.

We, humans, believe we are invincible; we're not. The dark entities never have to wait to find their next victim. These beings are on every street corner, in every home and business.

Demons plant seeds of discontent, anger, envy, and jealousy; they excel at creating chaos from order. They have a veritable smorgasbord of humans to feast upon every day. They laugh at our stupidity and enjoy frightening us. Most people can't see, hear or feel them, and the ones that can are afraid and won't interact with them. When things begin to go awry, we blame bad luck, Mercury retrograde, or another person instead of looking for a root cause.

Humankind is under the misconception that nothing on the physical plane of existence can stop the negatives from doing what they want in the physical world. Most think the only thing standing between the living and the negatives are holy men. But they are wrong; God has sent archangels and warrior angels into our world to create an army of lightworkers. These angels whisper in people's ears putting thoughts, ideas, images, and feelings into their minds. They do this to guide, inform and protect the living from the negatives in the world.

Angels in energy form walk among us, and angels are also born into physical bodies. The ones born into physical bodies are here to create a legion of lightworkers whose job is to spread the light among the living. The archangels who are reborn each have a mission to help humanity.

What's stopping the influence of the dark entities? Nothing, humans, are so easy to influence that it takes little effort on their part. Trip someone here, cause an argument there, create chaos from order.

Are the humans remotely aware of what's happening? I don't think so. Possibly some are, but most are not. Is God ignoring what is going on? No, I think He is waiting for humans to wake up and start helping themselves. We seem to expect God to do it all for us.

Why bother saving a drowning man if the man doesn't care or want to be rescued? What's the point? You drag him in from the tidal wave to dry ground, and what does he do? He whips out his iPhone and takes a selfie proclaiming his awesomeness at rescuing himself from certain death. What's the point if he won't do the work to save himself? He would much rather have someone else do the work for him.

You can see humanity slowly drifting away from God if you look closely. The church used to teach people to fear the wrath of God and the fires of hell. But times change, and people think it doesn't matter what problems, pain, and suffering they cause in the physical world. After all, they don't need to answer for it when they are alive, so why should they care.

GOD HEARS US

No matter how much the darkness tries to push back the light, it will never succeed. The darkness does not want to have its secrets revealed. The negatives want us to remain ignorant about them because the less we know, the greater our fear. Our fear feeds them and makes us vulnerable to their influence.

God has sent his warrior angels into the physical world. Some of these warrior angels are reborn into physical bodies, while others walk unseen among the living. The warrior angels who are reborn into physical form are lightworkers. The lightworkers have to bring light into the world to banish the darkness. When the light banishes the darkness, everything about the darkness is revealed. These warrior angels are creating a network of lightworkers, which has spread worldwide. The network of lightworkers grows daily, and the light shines more brightly than ever before.

God did not stop sending the warrior angels; he also gave the world the gift of eight archangels. These archangels have been reborn into physical form to fight a spiritual war. Most people think that the angels and their physical bodies are two separate entities, one residing in the heavenly realm and one in the physical body.

This is not how the soul, the archangel, resides in the physical body and remains connected to the heavenly realm. It amounts to having one foot in the physical world and one in the heavenly realm.

These archangels are demon slayers, healers, warriors, and avenging angels. They are an elite fighting team able to destroy demons of any caliber. Techalon, Haniel, Auriel, Celo, Elicita, Melitis, and Bartholomew. There are two in the United States, two in the UK, one in France and Italy, one in Canada, and one in South America. All are aware of who and what resides within them and are doing God's work.

The archangel within each physical body has powers that come directly from the white light realm. They can do everything from healing to killing demons. The physical body has a difficult time containing its power. The angel uses the physical body to cloak itself from being discovered by the dark entities. Typically, like most people, demons only look at the surface, never what lies beneath the physical body, which allows the archangels who reside within the physical body to remain hidden until they are called to action. This action would be to remove or destroy a negative entity. It works quite well for removing demons because it is too late for the demon to escape once the angel comes forward.

Most people think God does not hear their prayers or cries for help, but He hears every person. It does not matter if you whisper, shout, swear or think it. He hears all our prayers and pleas for help. Sometimes when we seek help, the time is not right to receive the help. By this, I mean either we have not learned the lesson or have not found the right person to help us.

Every adverse situation is meant to happen to teach us something. It is up to us to learn and take the lesson to heart. As humans, we do not always see the value of the lessons when they occur. Later, when we look back, most of us understand the need for the lesson and why we had to go through the situation.

God has said, "I don't have to punish you; you humans are pretty good at messing up your life all by yourselves." as humans, we tend to think if we don't get an immediate answer that, God has forsaken us or that he is disappointed in us. We never think that perhaps our problem is our own making. However, if you stop to think about the situation, you will see that something we did or did not do brought about it.

Humans also do not understand that time, as we know it, does not exist in the light or dark realm. So, if we ask for something to happen in a month, you might save your breath because they don't know how long a month is.

It all depends on your perception. Over there, what we think of as time moves slower in some respects and faster in other situations. Here is an example: When I died in a motorcycle accident, I was clinically dead for two minutes, but on the other side, it seemed like I was gone for a longer period. When I returned to my body, I thought I had been gone for hours.

No matter how we screw up or yell at Him, God forgives us. He can forgive us because he looks into our hearts and sees the hurt, anger, pain, and desperation that brought us to that point.

He told me a long time ago that He judges us by our heart, not necessarily our actions. As it says in the Bible: "It is not that which goeth into the mouth defileth a man; but that which proceedeth from the mouth, that defileth a man because it cometh from the heart."

God has no love or patience for the dark ones because they harm his earthly children and try to destroy His creation. He was wise to see that Lucifer was never happy with his position in God's kingdom. He knew Lucifer wanted to be the leader and would wait for the right time to strike. Therefore, He created the Legion of Light, which comprises the archangels: Michael, Gabriel, Raphael, and Auriel. These elite warrior archangels train the other angels who have a talent for using weapons, strategy, and warfare. In turn, these archangels train more archangels and warrior angels so that if there were trouble, they would step forward to defend the heavenly realm.

Another group of elite archangels called the Assassins were created to be covert operatives. They guard the throne of God and the door to the dark realm. They can cloak themselves from demons and other heavenly beings should the need arise.

After all, what do you do with elite snipers after the war is over? You keep them close to you, and should the need arise; they will be ready for battle.

There came a time when a division occurred among the souls in heaven. Some wanted to take on physical form to experience new sensations; others decided this was not for them. This was when Lucifer decided to go against God.

The battle began and lasted for what would be thousands of years in human time. In the end, the Legion of Light, the assassins, and the warrior angels defeated Lucifer and his followers.

After the war, the assassins were assigned as defenders of the heavenly realm. The warrior angels continued to train and be ready at all times. God hoped that never again would he have to call forth the assassins and the warrior angels to defend heaven. Although He has never had to call them forward to defend heaven, instead, they have been called into action to defend humanity.

Once the dark ones learned how to create dark portals and enter the human world, the warrior angels were activated. Once the demons had found their way into the physical world, they sent the warrior angels to walk among the living.

When the time was right, God selected the best of his warrior angels to be reborn into the physical world to create a network of lightworkers.

These lightworkers all had special abilities and could connect with the heavenly realm in physical form.

In the world today, there are more than 300,000 warrior angels in physical form using their abilities to help humanity. More than one million warrior angels are walking among us in spirit form.

As I write this book towards the end of 2021, a cosmic event has begun. It is an event that will last a year from start to finish. This event will bring prosperity, spiritual elevation, and the awakening of millions of lightworkers. It will also activate millions of warrior angels who are in physical form.

These warrior angels in physical form will benefit from the awakening by an increase in their abilities and a clearer connection to the white light realm. This will enable them to do their work in the physical world with greater ease. It will also bring awareness of the negative entities and how they work.

NEGATIVE AWARENESS

The fact that negative entities exist is something most people do not think about unless they encounter one. When they encounter one of these entities, they pass it off as their imagination, a trick of their eyes or mind, watching scary movies, or lack of sleep.

People believe negative encounters rarely happen in real life, only in scary movies. The people who believe this have never encountered a negative entity. These entities move behind the scenes like puppeteers manipulating individuals to do their will.

According to the Vatican, the number of people reporting demonic activity and possession has increased exponentially since 2013. On January 25, 2018, Newsweek published an article that said: The Vatican is training more exorcists than ever before in their history, as demonic possessions are soaring.

Negatives seek out people in key roles in the world to destroy and cripple man's way of life. Their goal is to cause wars, famine, disease, hate, anger, selfishness, jealousy, financial ruin, and destruction of the world, people, animals, and life itself. They do this because each human contains a white light soul, exacting revenge for God banishing them to the dark realm.

The people these entities choose are not random targets. These people are in positions of influence, power, money, and connections. The negatives choose their victims, carefully picking those who can do the most damage to the world. To become one of their puppets, you must meet certain criteria.

- Have power over financial institutions.
- Healthcare- (Big pharma).
- Economics- (people's jobs).
- The Military.
- Technology.
- Religious leaders.

If you look at the world leaders and people who work closely with them, you can see the shift. Negative entities can influence these individuals to make decisions that may bring about man's destruction. They use men and women of money and power to create discord, pain, and suffering.

Even clergy are not exempt from their influence. After all, what better way to control people if not through their religious leaders?

God is counteracting their moves by putting his people in places of power and influence. He watches the negatives carefully for signs of intercessions. Some seek to return to the light. Others attempt to do what needs to be done to earn their way back into the light. God has eyes and ears in the dark realm.

I can see what is happening on both sides, and to me, it looks like a global chess game with the light and dark realms moving the pieces. By pieces, I mean humans; we are pawns in this cosmic war. Some of us are willing participants, while others do not even know they are being used.

When the dark ones pick an individual as a target, you can literally sit back and watch the person change from a warm, giving, compassionate and caring person to one with no compassion, caring, or morals. They become filled with anger, hate, lust, and greed. Thus, begins this chain of events that will add to or propagate a negative way of being.

Most people are too busy living their lives to notice the subtle changes in an individual; they think the person is just going through something, and they will be fine. It is difficult for most people to see what is happening to them, and it is too late by then.

Here are some common misconceptions regarding negative entities:

- Negative entities are a rarity.
- They never come into the earthly plane.
- They cannot hurt you.

- If your faith is strong, you will never encounter a negative entity.

- The entities are only attracted to bad people.
- If you do not believe in them, they will not bother you.
- Crystals, salt, the eye of Horus, and sage will protect you against negative entities.
- Negative entities have no power over humans.
- Negative entities do not exist.

There are more negative entities in the world right now than ever before. The poorest of people in the world have the greatest faith in God or, as some say, the one Great Consciousness.

TOOLS FOR COMMUNICATION

Here are some tools people use to communicate with the other realms of existence. Each of these opens a doorway to the spirit realm, which connects to both heaven and the dark realm. I am not saying that communicating with the other realms is bad, but you must be very careful.

- Use of a **pendulum** to communicate in simple yes or no answers.

- **Divining rods**- small metallic rods with grips, which allow the rods to move of their own volition when in the presence of spirit energy.

- **Digital or tape recorders-**used to Record EVPs (electronic voice phenomena) in response to questions to elicit a response from the spirit realm.

- Reading **Tarot or playing cards** for divination.

- **Scrying**- using a bowl of water, candle, crystal ball, or mirror to connect with the spirit realm by focusing on the object and blocking any external distractions.

- **Spirit boards**-also known as **Ouija boards**- using this board enables the spirits to spell out words and respond to questions from those using the board.

- **Séances**- this method uses a medium as a channeling device through which the spirit or entity speaks relays a message to the living.

Using any of the above tools opens a door between our world and the other realms of existence. Many people are unaware that a portal (door) opens when using these tools. Most are unaware that you need to close the portals after the communication is over. Those who do know sometimes forget to close the door, which is when negative entities can enter our world.

Humanity has no concept of what the dark forces are doing to the world, along with man's greed and lack of concern for the future. The negatives have made their way into every facet of our world, including economic, political, social, religious, entertainment, and foreign affairs, to name a few. They have insidious but effective ways to integrate themselves into your life and manipulate you using the power of suggestion and even physical manipulation.

They use their abilities to probe your mind to determine what motivates you. Is it power, money, control, or lust? They will influence you to do things you would normally be reluctant to do. Their sole goal is to make humanity suffer in any way possible.

They have certain criteria, which the individual must meet:

- The person must be easily influenced.

- Weak-willed.

- Is the person easily manipulated?

- Do they have a support system/ loner?

- Faith- does the person have a strong belief system.

- Do they seek power, money, sexual gratification, fame?

- Are they willing to lie, cheat, steal or abuse others for their betterment?

- Do they have a conscience, feel remorse or sympathy?

- Are they willing to kill to get what they want?

- Do they suffer from addiction? i.e., drugs, gambling, sex, violence.

- Are they mentally or emotionally unstable?

- Were they raised, or are they living in an abusive situation, with violence, anger, jealousy?

Once they are certain the person is a prime candidate, the negative will start to insinuate itself into the person's life. The changes are subtle at first; then, gradually, the process continues until there are noticeable negative changes in the person's personality and way of thinking. Next, they isolate the person from their support system, i.e., family and friends. By doing so, it will make the person easier to control.

The upside is that there is hope, and God is aware of what is going on and has taken steps to counter their actions. At this moment, there are more Archangels and Warrior angels in physical form than ever before. There are eight powerful Archangels in a physical form whose job is to locate the demons and send them back into the dark realm or kill them. Warrior angels have come back as physical beings over the last seventy years. Their sole job is to bring awareness of these negatives and spread the word to the living. They teach the living what to look for and how to protect themselves.

NEGATIVE INFLUENCE

With so many people into paranormal investigating, is it any wonder that there has been an increase in paranormal activity? Most people are clueless that they create portals when they investigate and use their electronic devices to communicate. These portals allow the good souls and negative beings to come through into our world. While man tries to prove or disprove life after death, he opens thousands of active portals worldwide.

Humanity has no idea just how prevalent the dark ones are in the world today. They have very insidious ways of manipulating the living.

I hear from people almost daily how they have been suffering from an attachment or influence of a negative for weeks, months, and even years. This book aims to bring awareness to people about how influential these entities are in our everyday lives.

People always complain to me about there being no resources to help them. They are afraid to say anything to anyone because they think people will think they are crazy or trying to get attention. Even their own family won't believe what is happening until they are targeted. People fail to realize that if you have a demonic attachment, it doesn't affect just you; it affects anyone close to you. Everyone is a target, and everyone is in danger.

Even as we speak, they influence people of wealth and power who can do the most damage to the greatest number of people.

The consensus is that when you have a negative attachment, you are aware of it from the moment it happens; this is not always true. Negative entities are like stalkers; they wait and watch; they have all the time in the world. Here is how they work:
- They watch your daily routines.
- They observe your interactions with your family, friends, and work associates.
- What are your weaknesses, i.e., who you love, good friends, animals?
- What are your strengths?
- How easily are you influenced?
- Are you religious or not- how strong is your faith?

This stalking procedure can last for weeks, months, and even years. Once they have all the information, they begin to test you. It may start with just putting small thoughts in your head: i.e., not going to a party that you have looked forward to for a long time, waking up one morning feeling this inexplicable surge of hatred for your partner when they haven't done anything to warrant it. You may suddenly think that your partner is seeing someone else when there is no indication of this happening.

There are several ways they can influence people daily:

- Put thoughts in a person's head to self-harm, harm others, join satanic cults, and perform rituals to open a portal into the physical world.
- They can influence you to push the people closest to you out of your life so that you are alone and have no support system to help you.
- Drive when high or drunk, wreck your car, and kill someone.
- Torture and harm animals and children.
- They will influence you to become angry, jealous, bitter, augmentative, violent, depressed, withdrawn, and abusive.
- They can influence the choices you, make you take the wrong path. You must trust your gut instinct and choose to follow a different path.

Signs of influence:

- The person may feel like they are cursed or having continual bad luck.
- You may notice an infestation of dead insects, rodents, and even birds
- They may experience a sudden onset of health issues that have always had good health before. You may experience insomnia, nightmares, fatigue, and feel sick all the time. You wake up with

bruises, scratches, burn marks, and cannot concentrate.
- Your finances may take a drastic turn for the worse
- Relationships may become violent and abusive- their partner may feel like the person's personality has changed completely in a negative way.
- You can experience a false sense of security. You think you have gotten rid of them, and everything goes quiet, then the activity begins again.
- Things breaking-You can suddenly have a string of problems such as items breaking for no reason: large appliances, small appliances, computers, cameras, cell phones, landlines, watches, water heaters, building problems: i.e., roof caving in, electrical issues, water issues, car problems: i.e., dead batteries, belts breaking, the car won't start.
- Objects moving-Cabinet drawers, doors opening, furniture being tipped over, items stacked, objects suddenly disappearing and reappearing. Items are moving in front of you.
  .
- They can make people and animals perceive you differently. You find yourself suddenly unliked, and no one wants to be around you.

- You experience the loss of friends and family. Your pets no longer want to be near you; they act fearful when you are around.
- They can make you see, smell and hear things that aren't there. They can influence you to do things you wouldn't normally do. Mess with your mind to make you think you are going crazy.

What attracts the negatives to a person?

Here are a few examples of what attracts negatives.

- Substance abuse: alcohol and drugs.
- Satanic rituals.
- Reading and researching about the dark ones with the intent to contact a demon.
- A party where substance abuse is prevalent.
- Paranormal investigation in a haunted location.
- Obsession with communicating using EVP's, Ouija board, séance.
- You join a cult that encourages you to worship a person instead of a positive greater power.

- Clutter and chaos in a person's life is also a factor.
- Being obsessed with television programs about demons and dark forces.
- Emotional and mental instability.
- Violent or abusive personality.
- Living in a violent, abusive, or unstable home.

What you can do to help yourself

Do an impromptu EVP session and see what you pick up. If you get a negative response, stop doing the EVPs and call a reputable paranormal team.

If you suspect you have something negative in your home:

- Call in a paranormal team to see what they find.
- Prayer is a powerful weapon against negative's, but most of the time, you will need physical world help
- If you suspect you might have a negative attachment, reach out to your church
- If you don't have a church, reach out to local clergy. If this doesn't work, reach out to a demonologist or deliverance minister.
- If you cannot find anyone who will either believe you or help you, then contact me for help.

- A few of the most frequently asked questions that I receive is:
- What attracted the entity to me?
- Where was I when I acquired the entity?
- Why me? Am I a bad person?

Several things may attract a negative entity to a person, such as:
- You are in the wrong place at the right time.
- Substance abuse.
- You are in an abusive relationship.
- You have no strong belief system.
- Satanic worship.
- Unprotected spirit communication
- You exist in physical clutter and chaos.

You can acquire an attachment almost anywhere at any time. There is no rhyme or reason to when and where the attachment happens.
- Visiting friends.
- Doing EVPs.
- During a paranormal investigation.
- Visiting a cemetery.
- Abandoned buildings.
- Parties where alcohol and illegal substances are used.
- Just walking down a street.
- Spirit communication- receiving an intuitive reading.
- Using divination tools.
- Visiting a hospital or care facility.

Contrary to popular belief, you do not have to do anything to attract the attention of negative entities. Here are some reasons:

- You may be at a low point in your life.
- Going through trauma or stressful time.
- Loss of a loved one or beloved pet.
- You have a person close to you who is dabbling in dark practices.
- You are a lightworker.

DEMON THINKING

People think that demoniacs are all the same; they are not. They all have the same plan, to do as much damage to the person and their life as possible. But each of these entities has its own personality. Most are stubborn, tenacious, evil, and intent on punishing white light souls for what they see as their betrayal.

The Old Ones are the oldest and most powerful of the negatives, as I call them. They have been around the longest and are smarter than the lesser demons. These entities rarely come into our world; they cannot be bothered with us.

The only time I have encountered them in the physical world is either because they have been interred in the ground, ruined someone of importance, or have been sent to give an ultimatum to someone.

In response to the old demons' interference, archangels have been sent to do battle with them to stop their encroachment into the physical world. It takes an archangel to defeat an old demon, 'a titan against a titan'.

The Lesser demons are like hormonal teenagers, quick to act and judge a person simply by the external appearance alone, never looking any deeper than the surface. They think that all mortals are the same and base their strategy on that. These are the ones you will find mostly in the physical world attached to the living or influencing people to turn against the light.

To counter their interference, God has sent warrior angels into the world to observe them and take action when required. They can decide whether to send the demon back into the dark realm or kill it. They will exact revenge in their own way. God sets down rules and guidelines to help the angels make judgment calls when it comes to the punishment of the demons. If humans are involved, i.e., summoning demons, this judgment passes to the Legion of Light.

It's hard for the normal person to fathom how these entities work, but long story short, it's all about influencing your mind. Negatives will observe a prospective victim for some time to see if you are worthy of their time and energy. If they decide the person is not worthy of their attention, they move on, and you may never know what a narrow escape you had.

The person it chooses is easily influenced and may have physical, emotional, mental, or abuse issues. This makes them easier to influence and control.

Having decided to attach themselves to the person, they will choose one of a few ways to influence them.

They may find a memory of someone close to the person who has died and show themselves as an image of that loved one. The negative does this to gain the person's trust. Once they have gained their trust, they will start influencing them to do things they would not normally do. They may try to get them to break the law, hurt someone or themselves, steal, do drugs, and even in extreme cases, kill someone or take their own life.

Sometimes they will enter the person's dreams and create nightmares, physically attack them in their dreams and keep them from sleeping. It may begin as short scary dreams once in a while, and then the dreams will become more frequent and increase in duration, intensity, and frequency.

They will reach into the person's mind and find the image of what a demon should look like and amplify it a hundred-fold. The negative will then start showing itself to the individual in that form while they are asleep. They want to elicit fear from the person; this emotion feeds them and makes them stronger. Then they amp it up and start attacking the person while awake.

Whatever method they use, their goal is to isolate you from anyone, and everyone in your life ruins you emotionally, mentally, physically, and financially. They want you to lose what faith you have and turn your back on the light (God or whatever deity you relate to).

Prayer is a powerful weapon in the war against the darkness. Your body can be your best tool to let you know when something negative is around, and if you have animals, they will alert you by not wanting to go into a room, or they will growl at what you perceive as nothing.

I am here to tell you attachments do happen; the negatives choose their victims carefully. So, if you find yourself having issues, find someone who can help: clergy, demonologist (make sure they are reputable), or someone like me who specializes in negative entity removals. Never try to do it alone; get help. Because when you try to do it yourself, that's when they know they have won.

Not many people know that negative entities can use and control earthbound spirits to do their dirty work. A negative entity can prevent a human spirit from ascending into the light if it is present at the time of the body's death. The negatives use the earthbound spirits (ghosts) when they believe it will serve their purpose when a dark entity encounters an obstacle such as clergy, black salt, a house sealed with anointing oil, or holy water. They will use earthbound spirit to infiltrate the living person's environment.

Once the earthbound spirits' usefulness has ended, they will throw them away like garbage. The spirit must find a white light portal or a medium to help them cross into the heavenly realm.

Negatives cannot break through the barriers created by these holy items. Instead, they will use the earthbound to give the living nightmares, physically attack them, make them sick or influence the person to do things they wouldn't normally do. Once the usefulness of the earthbound spirit is over, they will discard them.

If you believe you have a negative presence in your house, you will know by saging the home or the area involved. This will indicate to the negatives that you are aware of them and trying to remove them. This is the last resort, and I advise against doing this except as a last resort. This is the last resort because the paranormal activity will pick up exponentially. Saging will not get rid of the negative it will only make them angry, and they will seek revenge against you for your attempt to get rid of them.

I would never advise anyone to try to banish a negative entity if they do not know what they are doing. If you try to remove it yourself, it will only backfire, and you can attract other negatives. You must enlist the help of clergy, a deliverance minister, or a demonologist.

Once you are sure the negative is removed from the location or person, you need to sage and lay down a black salt or holy water line. If you seal the location and are not sure the negative is gone, you will be effectively sealing it in with you.

Using sage will help clear any negative energy left behind by the negative entity.

You will also need to do a white light cleansing on yourself, your home, and even your animals. You do the cleansing because even after the removal is done, there are traces of negative energy within your body, home, and animals, which may attract other negative entities.

HOW DEMONS WORK

All demons have their own vibrational frequency. Each demonic type has a different frequency. Each is slightly different from the other, but the frequency is always in the low range.

The vibrational frequency of people who have mental health, drug abuse, low self-esteem, are physically or emotionally battered, or are in an abusive situation is different from those who don't have any of these issues. The negatives are drawn to these people because they know they are weak from their suffering. Demons use the little creepy crawlies minions to find suitable candidates for attachment. Once the entity finds a victim, they watch for weaknesses, instability, mental and emotional deficits. These use what they find to work their way into the person's mind and emotions until they wear them down and the entity has complete control over them.

These creatures are very methodical in what they do. They will sit back and observe the person, their actions, mannerisms, routines, relationships, thoughts, and beliefs. In this respect, the negatives are utterly patient.

I will tell you about them that are not commonly known because they are perfectionists; yes, they are absolute perfectionists.

They do not like to make mistakes and, therefore, will examine and observe intended targets until they are absolutely certain that they have all of the information they require to make that person's life a living hell.

There are different types of negatives; they usually fall into four main categories:

Old demons- the oldest and wisest of the demons. They remind me of mob bosses: ruthless, cunning, and demanding respect from the younger lesser demons.

Lesser demons- are like hormonal teenagers: they want to cause destruction, mayhem, and chaos for the living and angelic realm. They have little respect for the old ones in general. All they respect is power, strength, cunning, and violence.

Minions- shadow people, creepy crawlies to include **Wildcards** – banshees, Incubus, Succubus, watchers.

MINIONS:

Creepy crawlies are the followers and grunts of their realm. They follow the demons around like pilot fish follow sharks. They get no respect from the demons or other creatures of darkness. They travel in packs seeking out likely victims for the demons to attach themselves to and report to the demon.

***Shadow people*-**These creatures are loaners; they prefer their own territory. It is rare to find more than one in a location. They seek out the very young, old, and the infirmed, as they are easy prey for these creatures. They prefer those who have mental, emotional, and substance abuse issues. Their victims experience nightmares, fatigue, shortness of breath, and heart issues. They can suck the life out of a person and stop your heart. It will look like you had a heart attack.

Demons have all kinds of tricks to keep you from getting help. At first, they may make you think that you are hallucinating or hearing things. They may try to convince you that you are going crazy, or it's all in your head. The negative entities can make you see, hear, feel, smell and even taste things that don't really exist.

You're the only one who can see or hear what's happening for the most part. They do this to make you doubt yourself and your own sanity. Those around you may not see or hear any of this at first and wonder if you are having a nervous breakdown. Demons are great manipulators and love to play these mind games with the individual and those around them.

The negatives are all about isolating the individual and making those closest to them doubt their own sanity.

Demons can and do interfere and manipulate all kinds of electronic devices. They can even travel through telephone lines because it uses static electricity. They can make certain your emails do not go through to the person you seek help from. Using social media can ensure that your message is never seen or completely ignored by the person the message is meant.

When the person sending the message doesn't respond to their Facebook message, email, or phone message, they might think the person does not wish to help them, and they lose hope. When the person loses hope, it's easier for the negative to take over their life completely.

It doesn't matter if it's a cell phone or a landline; it's all the same as a negative; they know how to manipulate these devices.

I have even had them interfere with podcasts that I have done; after one podcast, the demons completely crashed the individual's recording system, including computers and phones. They are not above talking or growling in the background on recordings of some of the podcasts I have done.

I have had several cases where I never received a person's e-mail or Facebook message until months or even years after they were sent. It's no one's fault but the demons. They want to maintain their hold on the individual and do not want anyone interfering. They want the individual to believe that no one can help them, and they are constantly telling the individual this. If a person hears this long enough, they may soon believe it's true.

But what the negatives hadn't counted on is the guides and guardians of the person will manipulate circumstances and events to get the person help from someone who can get rid of the demons. The guides and guardians are not strong enough to stop the demons because they are common souls. They may go about it in a roundabout way because they are not as strong as the demons, but they are a hundred times smarter!

They do this by making something pop up on your computer, phone, radio, or a friend relays the information merely by accident (there is no such thing as coincidence).

Negatives can alter your perception and make you change your mind about seeking help. They can make you change your mind about finding help. They can put so many roadblocks in your way that you feel there is no way out and no one to help. People have been known to sink into a deep depression or decide to give up altogether and end their life.

It is very easy for demons to alter people's minds; it's second nature to them. It's a part of their arsenal of tricks that they use on humans. Humans are so into our heads that we forget to listen to gut instinct, which is our soul connection.

However, all is not lost; the angels and guardian angels use tricks in their arsenal to get us help. The angels may suddenly pull up my name or someone else's name to help the person. The angels will move people and things around to get you the needed help. The help may come unexpectedly and from quite an unexpected source. Something may pop up on your computer with someone's name or a podcast interview that pertains to your situation. It is all about perspective and being open to the possibility of something beyond your own belief system. As Shakespeare reminded us, 'There are more things in heaven and earth Horatio than are dreamt of in your philosophy.

Everything happens when it's supposed to happen and not a moment before. Maybe you didn't get help sooner because you were not ready when the first message or e-mail was sent. It could have been that you did not need the help as badly as you do now. It's all about timing and how great the need is for help.

HIERARCHY

Do beings of light and dark exist? If they do exist, what is their purpose? Do they have jobs in their respective realms? Why do they appear to the living? Do they intervene in our lives for a particular purpose? Is there a kind of uneasy truce between the light and dark beings? Why do the dark beings seek to harm the living? Does God have an army on his side? Why hasn't he simply gotten rid of the dark beings? Are the dark beings completely negative, or is there some spark of light buried deep inside them? Is there a hierarchy in heaven and hell, and if so, what is it? Is there mutual respect between the light and dark realms?

You may not agree with everything you read in this book, but at least it will make you think. Yes, there is a hierarchy and code of behavior in light and dark realms. This hierarchy has been in place for millions of years, along with a kind of uneasy truce.

Light Realm hierarchy is as follows:

- God.
- Jesus.
- Archangels include Demon Slayers, Assassins (hitmen), Avenging angels (the Legion of Light).
- Warrior angels.
- Cherubim and seraphim.
- Worker angels- worker bees.
- Guardian angels/ Spirit Guides.

The Dark Realm Hierarchy:

- Lucifer.
- His son M******.
- Second in command (we will call him George).
- George's lieutenant.
- Old demons–equivalent to archangels).
- Lesser demons-equivalent to worker angels.
- Minions- Shadow people, creepy crawlies.

Wild cards:

- Evolving demons
- The watchers.
- Succubus-Incubus.

Dark realm code of ethics:

- Humans are fair game.
- Lightworkers and clergy are prized (they want to torture and turn them into the darkness).
- God, Jesus, and the Archangels are to be respected by all, but only Lucifer and the old demons seem to follow this code.
- The other angels are to be harassed and, if possible, killed.

It rather reminds me of the Italian mob- if you are out for revenge on an individual, you do not bother the wife and children, and your target is the man.

Light Realm code of ethics:

➢ The white light souls that inhabit human bodies must be protected from the dark realm.
➢ If a dark entity is harassing the living, the entity must be returned to the dark realm.
➢ If a dark entity influences an act of genocide, then the offending entity will be eradicated for its crimes.
➢ If a dark entity influences the living to kill, it will be destroyed.
➢ The balance between the dark and light realms must be maintained.

Dark Entity Motivation:

After hundreds of thousands of years in the dark void, the fallen angels have grown vengeful and seek to exact their revenge when the souls are at their most vulnerable, in a physical body. The dark entity's whole goal in attacking the living is because inside each person resides a white light soul. They seek revenge on the white light souls because they were the ones who helped to send them into the endless dark void from which there is no true escape.

They have another motive for harassing the living, turning them away from the light and towards the dark way of thinking. They attempt to influence the living to create chaos, uncertainty, anxiety, instability, and worldwide fear and panic. They are all about bringing the end of the human race. They don't have to work too hard at it as we humans are easily influenced and can screw up our own lives.

Angelic Motivation:

Angels are all about letting the souls experience everything they can while in the physical body. They do not control the soul's life in the physical world, but they can offer advice, motivation and help the soul when they have lost their way. They know there will be times when the soul will want to experience the bad as well as the good.

Some people tell me they have asked angels to help them and seem to get no heavenly help. The angels will only intercede when the soul calls out for help. The physical body may see what is happening to them as detrimental, but the soul is committed to experiencing what the physical person may think is horrible. It is all about what the soul wishes to experience, no matter what we as humans may think. These good and bad experiences help us grow both in the physical world and on the angelic plane of existence.

EVOLUTION OF ANGELS AND DEMONS

It is a little-known fact that angels and demons evolve. With angels, the evolution is usually favorable.

With demons, it is usually unfavorable. It not only affects them physically but mentally as well. I have encountered some which seem to devolve. They tend to become mentally unstable, almost like a split personality.

The first one I encountered was over ten years ago. It was a creepy crawly which physically resembled a half-banshee, half-creepy crawly minion. Its behavior had changed; it behaved erratically and deviated from the standard demon behavior. Reaching into its mind, I found chaos and an inability to keep its thoughts on track. It had trouble relating to the other demons. Even its telepathic vocalizations changed to a high-pitched wailing.

The next one I encountered appeared to be mentally ill; if it were a human, I would say it was a sociopath. Even the other demons were shunned. When Lucifer found out about the demon, he ordered it destroyed.

These aberrations are far and few between, but when I find them, I notify the archangels, and they take care of it.

When angels evolve, they grow in power, strength, and wisdom. They are also growing to understand man's feelings and life stressors. Since they have not lived in the physical world, it is difficult to understand our day-to-day stress, worry, anxiety, and the need to make money to survive.

INSIDE INFORMATION

There are unseen forces all around you: in your home, work, literally everywhere- both good and bad.

The forces I am speaking of are demons and angels.

Demons:

Rogue demons- have no respect for Lucifer or any other demons. They have their own agenda, which does not include following the rules of the dark realm. Lucifer has created a special task force to track them down. He feels they are a threat to his rule. He has even gone so far as to ask Auriel for help. He has great respect for her ability to track them down and kill them. Lucifer doesn't like that he has no control over the rogues.

The old demons have great respect for the Legion of Light even though they are enemies. Lucifer and archangel Haniel were close friends before the war; Even now, he bears no malice because he chose to fight on the side of light. Haniel has been reborn into a physical body, Andy (referred to by the angels as the shell). He visits Haniel from time to time, and the body in which Haniel resides can see and interact with him.

The person, Andy, tolerates his visits but does not fully trust him.

Demons and angels are a mixture of good and bad. Angels have 1% darkness in them, and demons have 1% light. Something may trigger the light in a dark entity with demons, but they quickly squish it down. Occasionally the light will not be squashed, and it will grow. Then the demon must choose who to serve. The other demons ostracize those who choose to serve the light.

Demons cannot enter the light realm, but they can enter the earthly realm. The dark realm has sympathizers who still reside in the light. They are kind of like cold war sleeper cells.

Archangels:

They have a great sense of humor and are tenacious, stubborn, powerful, and are elite warriors. They are the oldest and wisest of angels. Contrary to popular belief, they are not perfect. No soul is except possibly God and Jesus. They do not reincarnate if they can get away with it. Sometimes they are asked to take on physical form to accomplish a task for him.

Why do we incarnate? We relive physical lives to experience things that we have never experienced before. We learn from these lives, whether good or bad, and grow. We gain knowledge and greater insight into man, emotions, and reasoning.

Sometimes we incarnate to experience life as a bad person to experience what it's like to live that type of life.

What happens when we screw up? Judgment, limbo, soul death? We are judged by our hearts, not necessarily by our actions. The death of a soul rarely happens, even if it means leaving the soul in limbo for all eternity. God cherishes every white light soul, but in extreme cases, when all else has been tried, and still the soul will not change or ask for forgiveness, then God must render judgment.

The Archangels are the only ones who can enter the dark realm and return unscathed. When they do enter the dark realm, it is usually for a very specific reason, such as:

- Tracking down a rogue demon who has caused harm to the living.
- Bring a repentant demon home to the light.
- Dispense justice or retribution.
- By commanded of God.

Archangels have spies in the dark realm, which keep watch for problems and are apprised of problems that negatively affect the physical world.

What happens in the dark realm? Is there a type of jail or limbo in Hell?
There are only two options in the dark realm, Limbo and the dark abyss, which we call hell.

Limbo is a form of prison, kind of like solitary confinement. – White light souls who have done horrible things during their physical incarnation, such as murder, abuse, and torture, are confined here to reflect on what they have done. The purpose of this is to experience firsthand the horror that awaits them in the dark realm. If they do not change their attitude and mind after some time, they are released fully into the dark realm without returning to the light.

THE SOUL

1. Can the soul be split, or does it have to remain whole to function? The soul needs to remain whole. It can leave the body for short periods to visit the white light realm or visit someone here in the physical world. It can visit a person in their dreams, but it can sometimes appear as an apparition, like an earthbound spirit.

    a) A soul can fracture, but this usually only happens when the person is bad, and the soul knows it will be judged on the other side and fears it will end up in limbo.

2. Can we live in both the physical and spiritual worlds simultaneously?
    a) Yes, it is not easy, but it becomes second nature with enough practice. It's almost as if half of your mind is aware of what is happening in both realms.

3. Do soul mates (twin flames) exist, and what exactly does this mean?
    a) Soul mates do exist, but not everyone has one. We move into family groups with our soul mates in the white light realm.

4. When we incarnate, does our soul mate incarnate with us?

a. Not always does the soul mate choose to incarnate with us. They may choose to stay on the other side and help us from there to achieve our goals in the physical world.

b. When we incarnate together, we may have a very different relationship, such as mother, father, sister, or brother. Remember, it's all about the experience.

5. Is the soul perfect, or is it flawed?
   a) The soul is not perfect; we all have little quirks and idiosyncrasies. Just as in the physical world, we have our own characteristics, likes, dislikes, and we are determined to experience as much as we can in the physical world, whether it's considered 'good' or 'bad.'

6. Why does the soul hold onto lives where they were not good people?
   a. Why hold onto experiences that do not benefit or add to the soul's perfection? The soul can be a bit of a hoarder; it will hold on to a unique life experience no matter whether it is beneficial just because it is different.

   b) Unfortunately, this is not always a good thing because the issue we are holding on to may surface again. The problem can surface during another lifetime and cause problems.

7. Human consciousness vs. soul consciousness.

   a) Most humans are so busy struggling to survive in the physical world they forget about the soul connection, even if they know about it in the first place.

   b) The soul has a mind consciousness of its own separate from the physical body consciousness. If you can connect to your soul consciousness, you will tap into a world of information to help you in the physical world.

8. Is the human condition an illusion?

   a) No, it's not an illusion, merely an instrument for our souls to experience new sensations and to learn from them.

9. Judgment: what awaits us? Who judges us? By what measure are we judged?

   a. As God once told me, we must answer for harmful things we have done in the physical world, i.e., murder, abuse, especially if it harms another soul. But He also assured me He considers the intention in our hearts when the event occurs.

Most people believe that the soul is perfect and is without flaws. Having lived all my life with one foot in the physical world and one foot in the angelic realm, I can honestly say that is not true. Our souls have their own personality, which is blended with the physical consciousness. Just as we need to fulfill our goals and dreams, so does the soul. For the soul, it is all about experiencing new things. It is up to the soul if it wants to live a physical life; no one forces us.

Before we come down to live a new life, we make certain decisions:

- The date and time we are born
- The date and time of our death
- The method in which we die
- What we want to accomplish- i.e., doctor, lawyer, parent, husband-wife.

We live many different lives in the physical world. The reason behind living these lives is so that we may experience all manner of things, such as:

- Physical disabilities
- Birth
- Death- cancer, car accident, heart attack, being murdered, hanging, etc.

All the scope of emotions- love, fear, anger, jealousy, anxiety, wonder, amazement, etc.

- Physical and emotional love.
- Success/ failure.
- Loss of a loved one.
- Illness.
- Wealth/ poverty.
- The birth of a child.
- Mental illness.
- Physical disabilities and limitations.

Our souls have been so long in energy form that we have forgotten how to feel emotions. We had forgotten what it was like to have a physical form and be subject to the ravages of aging, illness, physical, mental disabilities, and limitations. We understood the concept of fear, love, worry, stress but not the actual emotions.

When you have not experienced these things for thousands of years, you tend to forget the feelings associated with the emotion. You also forget the physical body's limitations and how fragile it is. So virtually, everything is as if you were experiencing it for the first time.

The soul is not perfect, although it is striving for perfection. Some souls hold on to things they shouldn't, like a traumatic death, a life filled with adversity, revenge, physical and emotional pain, anger, loss of a loved one, mental illness, physical and emotional traumas.

We had physical form millions of years ago with some of the same issues we have now when we incarnate. Even then, we held onto things we should have let go of. Once we evolved into pure energy, we should have let go of old problems and hang-ups, but unfortunately, many of us held onto the things we should have released.

Over the years, I have found souls holding on to traumatic deaths, horrendous lives full of pain and suffering, which can influence current lifetimes in different ways. Here are some examples of how it can influence the current lifetime:

- Physical pain- you may have chronic low back pain for which doctors cannot find a cause. You have chronic neck pain- then you find out you were hung in a past life. Then you find out you died in a past life from being stabbed in the low back with a spear.

- You cannot lose weight or curb your appetite no matter how hard you try. You find out you starved to death in more than one past life.

- You have an obsessive need to visit a country or place. You find out you lived several lives in that country or place.

All of these things are held in the soul's consciousness, and if the soul does not relinquish these experiences, they may resurface in another life, causing problems as in my husband Dan's case.

My husband has always had an absolute fear of drowning but has never even had a slip in the bathtub, even as a child. He is a very logical person. He believes if he cannot touch, feel or see it, it doesn't exist. Here is an example of a death holding over to the current lifetime.

One morning ten years ago, my husband Dan came to me about a dream he had:

"I need to talk to you about something," Dan said.

"Alright, what's up?" I asked curiously.

"I had a weird dream last night; it's the third night in a row I've had it." He began hesitantly.

"Tell me about it.

"When the dream begins, I am on Arizona a ship sunk in Pearl Harbor. I am below deck in the Recreation room. I am walking through the water as you walk through the air. Several men were there: some were playing cards; others were deep in discussion. The big topic of discussion is why no one came for them. The men's bodies had been left sealed below decks. They died a horrible death, watching the water rising and knowing there was no escape. I realized these were my shipmates, and I had drowned. They never recovered any of the bodies; instead, they were remanded to the sea. The next moment, I am up on the Arizona monument, and I am running my finger down the list of casualties on Arizona. I am looking for my name; when I find it, I wake up." He finished with sadness and confusion in his voice.

"Sounds like you were one of those men who drowned. That would explain your unreasonable fear of drowning."

"Yes, it certainly would explain my fear of drowning. Can you go on the web and get me a list of men who died on the ship?" he asked.

'Sure, I'll do it tomorrow after work. I thought you didn't believe in this sort of stuff." I said with a grin.

"Well, I'll tell you something, what I experienced in the dream was all too real; I think it's made me a believer in past lives. I think it would make me feel better if I could find my name." He said.

The next day I printed off 18 pages of men who had died on the Arizona. I gave it to my husband to go over. Several minutes later, he brought the papers back to me. On page fifteen, he had circled a name.

"This is it; this is who I was." He said solemnly, handing me the papers.

I looked at the circled name, and it read Raymond Arthur Roby. There is no such thing as coincidence. I had named our son after my grandfather Ray Arthur.

So, as you can see, we tend to hold on to things that do not add to the soul's perfection. Instead of just holding on to the drowning experience, the soul held on to all of the emotions: fear, pain, the horror of the lungs filling with water as you slowly drown. Gasping for air, you find your lungs filling with water instead and then the loss of consciousness.

As God once told me, the reincarnation process is not without glitches, especially if the soul tends to hold on to things it should not. Therefore, as you can see, our souls are not perfect.

WHAT NOT TO DO

If you suspect something demonic in nature in your home, there are a few things you do not want to do.

1. First, you do not want to make them angry, provoke or irritate them in any way. A couple of the ways you can irritate them is by saging the location and bringing in paranormal investigators. You do not want to provoke them by yelling, challenging, telling them to get out, or calling them names.

2. If you are stupid enough to do any of these things, then you had better be prepared for full-on spiritual war. Ninety-nine percent of people are not prepared to confront something they cannot touch, feel or see. It is a no-win situation by anyone's definition.

3. If you get the demonic name for some strange reason, you never want to say it aloud. The reasoning behind this is that it thinks you are summoning it if you say its name. This will cause it to attach itself to you or someone at your party.

4. You never want to acknowledge when you think you see a negative entity. By

acknowledging it, you draw attention to yourself and make it notice you. That is the last thing you want to do because once they notice you, they will start stalking you.

5. Demons know your future; they can see if you are destined to be a lightworker. They can see almost all of your future, but they cannot see your death or what leads to your death. Their goal is to turn you away from the light to the darkness; this is their ultimate goal.

6. Negative entities are a lot like stalkers. Once they find a likely victim, they will sit back and observe the person. This observation may last for a few minutes, a few days, or even years. After all, they have all the time in the world. When they watch you, they look for your weaknesses, strengths, and desires. They check the strength of your faith, not only in yourself but also in God.

7. They watch to see what is important to you, such as a child, an animal, husband, or lover. These are all things that are chinks in your armor, and they use these weaknesses against you. If you have an animal that you love, they will torment the animal and, in some cases, kill it. If your child is your weakness, it will torment the child with bad dreams, small accidents, and

health issues and even show themselves in horrific manifestations.

8. Demons never travel alone; they travel in packs for the most part. The only one of the demonic creatures that travel alone is a shadow person. They like their own company and their own territory; they do not want any other negatives encroaching on their territory. If you find more than one shadow person in a building, you have a big problem.

9. People believe you have to pray or put up a crucifix in your home to make one of these creatures disappear. I wish it were as easy as that. Most of the time, all this will do is anger them and increase the activity. If you have one of the creepy crawlies running around, you could probably sage and get rid of it for a little while because they are weak-minded. Unfortunately, they are linked with demons; they are their eyes and ears. The demons use them to seek out likely candidates for the demons to torment.

10. People fail to realize that a demon or a ghost, for that matter, can make you see them as they wish to be seen. They will try to show themselves as something horrible that will totally incapacitate you with terror and fear. Most people cannot seem to get past that point.

These negative entities are used to being perceived with absolute terror. This is what they strive for; they want to make you so terrified that you're unable to think and act coherently. They want to incapacitate you.

DOORWAYS INTO OUR WORLD

Portals are doorways or openings to other dimensions. There are different types of portals:

- Some are naturally occurring due to high electromagnetic energy fields.
- Some are created by man, most of the time not intentionally.
- Negative entities create some
- While others are created by light beings, i.e., angels.

Here are some of the ways humans create portals:

- Using divination tools such as tarot cards, scrying, divining rods, intuitive readings.
- Séance's, Ouija boards.
- Satanic rituals for summoning the dead or demons.

Before you use any of the above tools for communication with the spirit world, you will need to as for God's blessing (or whatever deity you believe in) on the communication. After the communication, you must ask God to close and seal the portal.

The problem is that these portals are left open. An open portal can and does attract both light and dark beings.

All man-made portals need to be closed after use. Very few people know you need to close the portals after completing your communication. Most of the time, they do not even know they have opened, let alone created one when doing a paranormal investigation or an EVP session. It's time people were educated about the repercussions of what they are doing.

If you do not close the portal, anything and everything will utilize it to enter our world. This often leads to hauntings and demonic infestation. The last thing you want is negative entities populating our world and terrorizing the living.

The paranormal activity is always negative, i.e., physical attacks, sudden bouts of anger, nightmares, feelings of foreboding, and the air may feel heavy and oppressive. You can tell if there is a dark portal near you by the amount of negative energy and dark entities encountered within a concentrated area. The negative entities like to stay close to where the portal is located. The closer you get to the portal, the more intense the activity.

They are easy enough to find if you know what to look for. Their vibrational signature is unique, unlike any other realm's frequencies. When you find one, you may experience:

- Dizziness,
- Nausea,
- A sick feeling in the pit of your stomach

- A sense of dread
- The atmosphere will feel oppressive

The problem is that these portals are opened but never closed. Leaving a portal open can and does attract both light and dark beings.

What should you do if you encounter a dark portal? Obviously, you need to get as far away from it as possible. The average human, even a strong psychic or medium, cannot close or move these portals. You must ask for divine intervention to protect you and close the portal.

HOW DEMONS MOVE THROUGH OUR WORLD

People have often asked me how a negative entity can move undetected in the physical world. There are a few ways that a negative entity can do this.

The negatives are hell-bent on entering our world to attack the white light souls who inhabit human bodies. The white light souls are most vulnerable when they are in human form. They are vulnerable physically, emotionally, mentally, and spiritually. We are at the mercy of our brain; we let our brain rule our life, talking us out of listening to our soul consciousness. People tend to forget a soul resides within the physical shell we call a body. It is older and wiser than any living person, and if we connect with the soul consciousness, then there is a wealth of information we can tap into.

Over years of dealing with negative entities, I have learned that they are tenacious, inventive, vengeful, OCD, coldly calculating, unforgiving, and driven by revenge. They seem to work overtime on finding ways to create incursions into the physical world.

They intend to invade or attack humans; they seem to be especially fond of sudden or brief repeated attacks. Here are a few of their favorite ways of entering our world:

- Dark portals- doorways created from the dark realm into the physical world.
- Vail rending- introduce smoke-like dark energy into your location to mess with

your mind and emotions, which can cause sleeplessness, mood swings, irritability, and fatigue.
- Tunnels- like the tunnels used by Viet Cong soldiers as hiding spots during combat, the demons use these tunnels to get around undetected.
- Humans- influencing humans to do dark ceremonies to summon demons.
- Portals can be opened by the use of: paranormal investigations, EVP sessions, divination, and spirit communication utilizing séances, Ouija boards, pendulums, divining rods, tarot cards, or even channeling.

Demons are nothing if not inventive; over the centuries, they have learned to utilize man's tools for communication to travel from one person to another. Demons can be stalking one person, and if that person has a friend who is trying to help them, the demon will travel from the person they are attached to and attack the other person utilizing one of the following:
- Phone (landlines).
- Cell phones.
- Electricity- electrical lines.
- Humans' bodies.
- Telegraphs.
- Battery-operated devices.

Anything that is battery operated or uses electricity in any form is a tool they can use.

Over the last forty years, I have discovered other ways the negative entities have traveled, which have nothing to do with electronics.

Recently I have discovered that negative entities have created tunnels under most of the landmasses in the world. They can use these tunnels to travel undetected from one spot to another. If you were to see the tunnels from above the earth, it would look like a giant red glowing spider web.

DEMONS ARE EVERYWHERE

People do not realize no matter where you are in the world, there are millions of angels, spirits, ghosts, and demons everywhere you go.

Here is an example of how it works. These entities are around us all of the time; you cannot go anywhere without their presence. Even most psychics and mediums only see or sense a few at a time. They come and go as they please, and most of the time, people do not see or sense their presence.

When someone has a ghost encounter, they usually only see one spirit at a time. Although there may be multiple spirits in the room, you do not see the rest of them. This is because the individual spirit may want you to see them. However, the other spirits in the room might not wish to engage with you. It is up to the individual spirit when and if they choose to reveal themselves to you.

Negative entities are like hyenas; they travel in packs. Where you find one, there will always be others close by. The exception to this is shadow people, incubus, and succubus. These particular entities like their own territory. They will not share with any of the other negatives, not even another of their own kind.

These negative entities move through our world at will, looking for the weak and unsuspecting. Old demons usually do not enter our world; they feel we are unworthy of their time and energy. On the rare occasions when they do enter our world, it is usually for one of two reasons,

> 1. Lucifer has given them a task to do for him. We are not talking about something minor; we are talking about something which will negatively affect the whole world.
> 2. Or they may be seeking revenge on a white-light soul who has wronged them.
> 3.

When the old demons are looking for a suitable person to use in a large-scale project, they are looking for someone with wealth, power, and influence in areas that will affect and damage the living.

The person needs to be susceptible to their influence have weaknesses that will drive them to do whatever it takes to get the job done. Once they have found their victim, they will devise a plan to utilize the person to cause as much pain and destruction as possible.

On the other hand, angels move through another realm of existence on a higher plane, one that most humans cannot perceive. The people who can see their realm are the ones who have an angelic soul that has been born into a physical body.

The warrior angels move silently among the living to watch the negatives. It is a full-time job and one that is very much needed. The warrior angels cannot be everywhere all the time, so God sends warrior angels back into the physical world to live mortal lives. These warriors act as God's eyes and ears here in the physical world. Even with all this due diligence, some negatives go undetected, and they attach or attack the living.

When humans cry out for help because of a negative entity attack, it is then that the message is carried to the archangels, who will send a warrior angel to see what is happening and report back to them. Sometimes it takes a while for the message to get to the archangels because the demons will try to interfere and keep it from getting through.

Both angels and demons can cloak themselves so they cannot be detected by each other if necessary.

OLD DEMONS

Dark beings move through the world using the cover of darkness as a shield, enabling them to travel among humans without being detected. Demons bring with them chaos, destruction, anger, and suffering. Humans are happy to remain in denial until they encounter one of these creatures. Most people cannot or will not see these beings, but those of us can see them. If you have no experience dealing with these creatures, it is wise to avoid them altogether.

Old demons were not always negative; they were once beings of light. They were some of the first to evolve into pure energy. They are very intelligent, powerful, cunning, and vindictive. In appearance, they are similar to archangels: seven feet tall, twelve-foot wingspan, but they are an ebony black, and their facial features are almost indistinguishable. The only feature you can make out in their face is the glowing yellow eyes. Lesser demons and minions all have red glowing eyes with the same evil in them.

If you look into these eyes, you will see a horrible evil that would chill you to the bone and give you nightmares for years to come. It actually hurts to look into their eyes. You will rarely find them in the physical world of their own violation unless it is to seek vengeance for a perceived wrong.

Battleground Demon

It was a Monday evening, and I was on my way home from work when my cell phone rang. I could see by the number that it was Dave, a friend of mine. When he calls me, it is usually because he has found something negative. Sometimes he gets a client who needs a little more help than he or his paranormal team can provide.

I answered the phone, and Dave said, "I've got this client, and we've already been out to his house a couple of times. There still seems to be a lot of activity there, and it feels very negative. Would you give him a call and see if you can help?"

"This is your specialty. Could you connect with him and see what you think," he asked a little uncertainly.

Smiling, I replied, "Alright, text me his number, and I'll call him later this week when I have a day off."

"Thanks, I know he needs help, and you would be helping me out too. I'll send you the info right away."

After I hung up the phone, I received a second call; this one was from Stuart, another friend.

"What are you doing on Sunday?" he asked.

"Nothing yet. Why, do you have something for me?"

"I got a call from a woman I met at the ghost conference. She wanted our group to do an investigation on her home. However, the thing is, she has already had two other groups come to the house. I do not feel another investigation would do any good. So, I asked her what the purpose of investigating again would be. It turns out that she wanted someone to talk to the spirits to find out who they are and what they want in her house," he said.

"Okay, so what do you want to do?"

"Would you be open to going with me and doing a walk-through to see what you can pick up? Maybe you can talk to the spirits and find out why they are there..."

"Sunday will work," I told him.

"Okay, I'll set it up and then let you know what time."

"Alright, I'll wait to hear from you."

This will be my second negative removal in less than a week. It seemed like there was an overabundance of negatives running around lately. I suddenly remembered the higher powers I connected with, saying that the Light was spreading worldwide.

The darkness is trying to keep the Light from spreading, causing an increase in negative activity. My guides had warned me that there would be peaks of negative activity over the next several years.

The next morning as I was getting ready for work, I felt one of my guardians connect with me.

"What's up?" I asked my guardian, Michael. "You usually don't physically show yourself. Something must be up," I said telepathically.

"Have you received the information from Dave yet? This negative is an incredibly old and a nasty one," Michael said telepathically.

Turning to look at him, I saw a gleam of anticipation in his eyes.

"Now wait just a minute; you knew this was going to happen, didn't you? I wouldn't be surprised if you put it into Dave's head to call me." Seeing the grin spread across his face, I knew what had happened. "You're going to owe me one for this, you know. Just for that, I will not call him until my day off on Wednesday. I only hope what is waiting for me in Hillsboro isn't a nasty old demon too. Cut me some slack here; we had that negative entity last Sunday."

"Don't worry; the surge in darkness is almost over for now, and then you can relax for a while," Michael said, looking disappointed.

"Gee, how terrible!" I said sarcastically, but he just grinned and disappeared.

Two days later, when I called and spoke to Dave's client, Tom, I said, "I understand you're having a lot of activity at your house?" As I connected with him, I could feel the presence of the negative.

"Yes, it's been going on since we moved into the house four years ago. I need someone to get rid of it. I can't take much more of this." He sounded like a man at the end of his rope.

"Dave told me his paranormal group came out to your house to investigate. He said he felt something dark there, but it's something he's unable to help you with."

"Yes, Dave told me that I needed to find someone capable of dealing with dark spirits, and he said that you are the best. Could you please help me get rid of whatever this thing is?"

"Yes, I'll help you. I can't come until Sunday because I work, and I have another person on Saturday who needs my help."

"That's fine. Whenever you can come is fine with me. Do you need me to do anything? Do you need any more information?" he asked.

"I don't need anything other than your address. I never like clients to give me any information. When I go into a place, I like to go with no preconceived ideas about what I might find."

"Alright, when can you come?" he asked.

"We'll try for 3 o'clock on Sunday if that's okay with you?"

"Sure, whenever you'd like ... the sooner, the better."

"Alright, I'll see you on Sunday," he said, sounding hopeful, and hung up the phone.

Sunday around noon Stuart and his wife arrived at my house. We talked for a few minutes about the woman's case. Then the conversation turned to later in the afternoon.

"So, you said you had another appointment this afternoon. What sort of appointment is it?" Stuart asked.

"Dave called me about a man who is having an issue with a demon in his home. I'm going there to do a walk-through and do the removal," I told them.

"Wow, is it all right if we go along? You might need someone to watch your back during the removal if there is a demon there," Stuart said seriously.

"I'd love to have you come along; I think he could use a minister," I said, smiling.

"What makes you think he needs a minister, besides the obvious?" he asked.

"Because he just texted me and asked if I was a Christian," I said, showing him the text on my phone. "That reminds me. I'd better text Tom to let him know we probably won't be there until after four."

After helping the woman with the entities in her house, we headed for Battleground, Washington, where Tom lives. It took us longer than I thought to get to his home because he lived in a rural area on the outskirts of town. The closer we got to the house, the more pronounced the negativity.

As we pulled into the driveway, Tom came out through the garage to greet us. I could sense the presence of an old and enormously powerful demon.

"June?" he said, holding out his hand.

Shaking his hand, I introduced Stuart and Tina to him.

"Stuart is the founder of the paranormal group I work with. He's also an ordained minister; I thought you might feel more comfortable with him here while I do what I need to do to remove the negative."

Shaking hands with Stuart and Tina, Tom said, "I just want you to know that before I started having these experiences, I didn't believe in this paranormal stuff. If I thought of it at all, I tended to think only bad people were attacked by negatives, not God-fearing people like my wife and myself. Now I know for sure these things are real. Thank you for coming."

Turning to me, Tom asked, "Do you want to start on the inside of the house or the outside?"

"I can feel it watching us and trying to figure out what we're up to. It's upstairs, so let's begin inside."

Following Tom into the house, I could sense three earthbound spirits trapped by the negative. As I entered the dining/ kitchen area, I could sense an older woman somewhere in the back of the house in the covered porch area. Moving towards that area, I saw the spirit of a young boy peeking at me from around the corner. Smiling at him, I spoke to him telepathically. "Hello, you don't have to be afraid. I am here to help you. I'm going to get rid of that nasty thing upstairs."

"Other people who came here said they would help, but they didn't. They just made it mad, and things got worse," the boy told me.

"Well, I have something they don't have," I told him.

Unexpectedly he smiled at me, "Yes, I know, I can feel it," he said and disappeared.

Coming back into the dining area, Tom was telling Stuart about the death of his wife a couple of years earlier.

"Before we bought the house, my wife never had a sick day in her life. She was always smiling and upbeat. After we moved in here, she began to experience health issues. At first, it was small things. Then about ten months later, she was diagnosed with a rare form of cancer and was dead within a year. The doctors told me they had never seen cancer so aggressive.

When she was ill, she would see dark mists, have horrible nightmares, and feel like something was trying to get her to kill herself. I just thought it was cancer taking its toll, but then I started seeing things, and I believed her," Tom told us, shaking his head in regret.

"You couldn't have known what it was. You had no experience with what she saw," I reassured him.

"It was shortly after her death that the activity got worse. It was then that I contacted Dave, and his paranormal group came in to investigate. After the first time, the activity settled down for a couple of days."

"The second time they came out, one of the women gave me four crystals to put in the four corners of the house. She told me that these crystals would protect me; they didn't. The first night I put the crystals in the corners of the house. The next morning, I found two of them lying on the kitchen table. The second time I put the crystals out, the one I had placed in my son's old room on the floor was broken in half."

"There's something negative here, but I have no idea where it came from. I'm depressed all the time, I have strange dreams, and things move. Something tried to pull me out of my bed on more than one occasion. No one wants to stay here, including me. I've been poked, scratched, heard voices, growling, and knocking. I don't know how much more I can take," Tom said, and I could hear the desperation and fear in his voice.

"That's what these things do," I said, "They try to beat you down, isolate you from your support system and ultimately ruin your life and relationships. Crystals can be used to amplify your psychic abilities and warn you of impending danger if you know what to look for. Unfortunately, they cannot protect you against negative. The person who gave you the crystals thought they would protect you. Even if they were able to, it wouldn't have solved the problem."

"It looks like you're in the middle of a moving sale," Tina commented, looking around.

"Yes, I can't stay here anymore; there are too many memories here for me," Tom replied.

"Your wife is still here; she died in this house, didn't she?" It was more of a statement than a question. "The negative is keeping her spirit trapped here in the home. It had something to do with her death. She may have had cancer, but this thing caused it and sapped what little strength she had left. You could say it killed her. She has been unable to cross over because it won't let her. She's trapped, and she wants you to know she helped you find me," I told him.

"I've always felt she was trapped here, but I didn't know what to do about it. I don't know how I knew she was trapped here, but I think it's the demon taunting me," Tom said with an angry look.

I looked at him with a serious face and told him, "The anger you have towards the demon is feeding it, helping it grow stronger. I'll bet you provoke it quite a bit, don't you?"

He looked me straight in the eye and admitted that he did. "Yes, I suppose I shouldn't have done that. I told that thing to stop bothering my wife. I told it if it wanted to pick on someone, it could pick on me. I thought if I gave it another target, it would leave her alone."

"It didn't work; instead, you let it know where your greatest weakness lies. It used your love for your family to its greatest advantage. Demons may not be very bright; you might even say they're stupid. By that, I mean they are a lot like some people, who only see the outward facade, never looking at what's inside. You should…." I stopped in mid-sentence sensing the negative moving around upstairs.

"Tom, you need to understand, if it is showing anger, then it has a weakness. We can use that weakness against it," I explained to him.

"How do we do that?" Tom wanted to know.

I just smiled at him and started towards the stairs.

"I'm going to start the recorder," Stuart said.

Nodding my head, I paused at the foot of the staircase. I could feel the demon trying to keep us from going up the stairs.

"The air feels thick here, and it's getting harder to breathe," Tina commented.

"Yes, I can feel a heaviness that wasn't there in the other room," Stuart agreed.

I looked at the others standing behind me, "It's going to try to stop us from getting up the stairs. I want you to be aware that it might get a little scary, but not to worry because we have protection," I said, looking meaningfully at them.

As I looked up toward the top of the stairs, I could see the demon standing there, trying to scare me by increasing its size and fierceness exponentially. It growled a warning to intimidate me into backing down. It grew from 6 feet to 8 feet with huge glowing red eyes and sharp white teeth.

"Ignorant bitch, insignificant mortal, you cannot help him. You can't stop me from doing whatever I want. I will make your life a living hell," it said telepathically, smiling evilly.

Returning its wicked smile, I sent it a telepathic message, *"Judge me by this physical body, do you? Stupid demon, which will be your downfall. You have no power over me or anyone anymore,"* I told it.

I sensed it lashing out at Tina. However, to call in the higher beings at this time would give my hand away. All I could do was extend my protection, a white light force field around her. Suddenly a surge of negative energy shot from the demon as it reached out and tried to push Tina down the stairs. Because she had my shield around her, the impact was lessened.

Opening my mind, I connected with the white light realm from which my gifts emanate.

Having failed to injure Tina, the demon reached its hand into Stuart's body and tried to stop his heart. I lashed out, stopping the demon's hand from crushing Stuart's heart.

"Stupid demon, you think you can stop me with your pathetic attempts to injure my friends? You have learned nothing in all your long years of existence, or you would know who I am!" Auriel told it, her voice full of disdain and disgust.

As I climbed the stairs towards the demon, I could feel the powerful white light energy filling my body, mind, and soul as archangel Auriel came forward. As the power of the light filled me, I could feel the demon trying to push my physical body back as I climbed the stairs. I watched as the demon's demeanor changed and a fleeting look of fear crossed what passed for a face. Surprise and disbelief quickly followed the fear.

"Stupid demon, know you not who I am?" I could hear Auriel ask.

"No, you are not supposed to be in the physical world," the demon screeched and started backing up as I moved towards it. It lashed out at me, sending a surge of negative energy towards me. Raising my hand, I deflected it.

I kept moving forward, herding it into a bedroom on the left at the top of the stairs. The demon became increasingly angry and combative. I could feel the others behind me as I entered the room. The white light power coursed through me as I held the demon contained within the room.

"Michael, Gabe now," I shouted telepathically. The archangels suddenly appeared behind the demon grabbing and holding on to it.

"Now, demon, tell me why you were entombed in the earth," I commanded.

"Never, if you are so smart, assassin, you figure it out," it growled.

"Demon, I command you in the name of all that is holy to answer my question!"

Unsheathing his white light sword, Michael held it at the demon's throat. *"Answer the question or pay the price for your disobedience,"* he said, drawing the sword tighter.

"I disobeyed Lucifer!" It snarled.

I cocked my head, considering the validity of the answer. *"There's more to it than that; I'll wager,"* I said telepathically, grinning at Michael.

He grinned in return, *"I believe you're right about that. Lucifer may have a nasty temper, but I've never known him to give out that kind of punishment for a paltry offense. No, it's got to be much bigger than that. Alright, give."*

"I was sent on an assignment to influence a priest to go against his vows. This wasn't just any priest," it said with an evil smile. *"This was the Pope, a particularly spineless one. I thought about it and then decided if Lucifer wanted it done, he*

could do it himself, and I told him so. Oh, you should have seen the look on his face; it was priceless. Unfortunately, he didn't like my answer and imprisoned me here on the earth. He said I needed to be reminded of who was in charge."

"You're lucky he didn't kill you. Too bad, I would have," Auriel said with relish. *"But I have something far better in mind."*

The demon looked at me suspiciously.

"I'm going to send you back to him as a present," Auriel informed it.

"You can't send me back! Lucifer said if I ever returned, he would make an example of me," it screeched at me in anger and fear.

"Too bad!" Michael said.

Holding the demon firmly between the two of them, Gabe and Michael delivered him to the dark world.

Moments later, Michael appeared beside me, *"Nice work. Feels like old times, doesn't it, Gabe?"*

"Yes, I do miss the old days," Gabe agreed.

The white light power that filled me subsided into the background of my mind, and I was once again in control. My body felt like it had been in a physical fight and lost.

"Is everything okay? What happened?" Stuart asked me.

"Yes, I'm okay." Taking a deep breath, I cleared the fog from my mind, and I relayed what had taken place to them. It seemed like it took at least an hour to remove the demon, but only a few minutes had passed in reality. Now I was being drawn towards the opposite end of the upstairs.

"There's an older man here, and he says he's your grandfather. He says his name is Giuseppe," I informed Tom.

"Yes, that's my grandfather who died in Italy. I never met him, though," Tom said.

"It doesn't matter that you've never met him. He is the older man you have seen in the house from time to time. He's one of your guardians, and he has been trying to protect you and your family from the demon. Unfortunately, he wasn't strong enough to do much. Now that the demon is gone, he will be able to help you get through this tough time. You're going to Italy, aren't you?" I asked.

"Yes, I'm selling the house and everything in it and taking a trip to Italy to see where my family came from. I'm not sure what I'm going to do when I get back."

"You'll return to Italy and stay there for a little while, then return," I told him. "Your wife is here; she wants me to tell you that she can ascend now. She says she loves you and for you not to worry about her. She'll be watching over you and be waiting for you when you cross."

"Thank you. Will you tell her I love her, and I'm glad she's going to be with God?"

"She can hear you whenever you talk to her, and when her name pops into your head, know that she's here with you," I assured him.

"Thank you. What about the old woman's and the boy's spirits that are here?" he wanted to know.

"They have been released and have ascended. Now I'm being drawn outside. Is it alright if we go out there now?" I asked Tom.

"Sure, sure, no problem. Let's go out the front door." Making our way back downstairs, he opened the front door.

Stepping outside, I felt a surge of energy coming from the backyard area. Following the energy trail, I found myself drawn towards a small shed at the backside of the property. The closer I got to it, the stronger the energy became.

Turning to look over my shoulder, I noticed everyone had followed me. "You have a portal here, but not just any portal." Seeing the question on his face, I explained. "A portal is like a door to another dimension. Some are good as they let the good spirits come and go as they please. Some portals are bad because they are created and used by negative entities to come and go from their world to ours. I call them dark portals. Then there is this kind which is allowing both good and bad to pass through; I'll have to do something about that."

Moving closer to the shed, I laid my hand on it and could feel the vibration caused by the humming of the portal. "If you want to feel something neat, come over here and lay your hand on this building," I invited them.

Stuart was the first to lay his hand on the building. "Wow! It's really vibrating; it sort of has an electrical quality about it. Tom, you have to feel this. It's weird and cool at the same time," he urged Tom.

"You're feeling the vibrations from the portal. Being more sensitive, I feel the same thing only magnified ten times," I said.

Tom laid his hand on the building and then remarked in a surprised voice, "You're right; it certainly is vibrating. I haven't been out here in a long time, and I guess that is why I never noticed it before. What does a portal look like, and what do we do about it letting in the negative ones?"

"If you can picture a tornado that is mostly white swirling around, that's what it looks like, and the dark portals look the same, except they are black or dark grey. I have to place a filter over the opening. It will prevent any more negatives from using it as a doorway into our world."

Looking at Stuart, I said, "If you place your hand on the door while I'm applying the filter, you can feel some of what I feel. The shed is sitting right on top of the portal opening."

"Wow!" he said, laying his hand on the door.

Closing my eyes, I placed a hand on the shed door and focused on creating a web-like film over the portal's opening. I could feel the power emanating from the portal. Concentrating, I increased the power flowing from my hands. As I did, I could feel the door on which my hand rested start to vibrate harder. I could hear broken glass rattle yet remain firmly in place. I could see the filter form and cover the portal's opening within my mind's eye. Once the filter was in place, I opened my eyes and saw Stuart and Tom next to me. Smiling at them, I asked, "Well, what do you think?"

"I'm telling you that the glass on the door was vibrating so much that I was afraid I might get cut by the loose glass. So, I took my hand away from the door before you finished," Tom remarked.

How did it go? Did you get the filter put in place?" Stuart questioned.

"Yes, it's in place now." Turning to look at Tom, I said, "You shouldn't have any more problems with negatives coming through the portal. Sometimes good spirits may come and go, but you shouldn't have any problems with them. If they happen to come into the house, just let them know that the house is off-limits.

They may come to you asking for help to cross over. Just tell them to look for the white light and then walk towards it. Let them know they'll find their loved ones in the light."

"Is that it; are you done?" Tom wanted to know.

"No, there are a couple of other things to take care of," I said. Turning towards the house, I could sense an elemental residing under the porch. I said, "You can come out now. The demon is gone, and there won't be any other negatives to bother you. However, you can't stay here; you need to return to the forest. That's where you belong."

"What's an elemental?" Tom asked curiously.

"Elementals are nature spirits; they are sometimes known as leprechauns, sprites, fairies, gnomes, or pixies. They are all spirits watching over the land, water, trees, rocks, and sacred sites such as Stonehenge. Your wooded area is where some of them live. They want people to take care of the earth and give back to it. Most of them are harmless enough, but a few have a mean streak in them.

They all can be mischievous and cause you problems if you don't respect the land, plants, animals, or waterways. This one is just nosey," I told him.

A funny, short little gnome-like creature crawled out from under the porch. "Are you sure I can't stay here? I like it here, and there are plenty of mischiefs to get into!" it said, laughing mischievously.

"No, I'm sorry you can't stay here. You need to return to the forest. That's where you belong, not here among humans," I told him telepathically.

"Alright, I'll go. Will you come and visit me?" he asked with a twinkle in his eye. I just smiled at him, but he didn't answer.

I watched as he scampered off into the woods. As he disappeared from view, I saw a group of Native Americans watching us. One of them stepped forward and spoke to me telepathically, "You are the one who removed the evil one?"

"Yes, it is gone for good now," I assured him.

Turning to the others, I let them know what was going on. "I just sent the elemental who was living under your house back to where he belongs in the woods. As he was leaving, a group of Native Americans appeared between those two trees in front of me." I said, nodding at the trees in front of me, "They want to make sure that the demon is gone, and I have just reassured them that it is gone. I think they want something more from me, so I need to talk to them."

"How do you know they're Native Americans?" Tom asked curiously.

"The Native Americans who used to live here are the keepers of the land."

"I guess I never thought about it. I think we take the land for granted and forget about giving back," Tom mused.

Turning my attention back to the group of Native Americans, I told Tom, "They are spirits who live and watch over the wooded area here behind your home. And they wish to speak with me. Is there something I can do to help you?" I asked the leader.

"We have been guarding the forest, which is our home. We have been trying to protect those in the home from the evil one, but it was too strong. We were told you would be coming to remove the evil one, so we watched and waited. You will protect this land?"

"Yes, I will give this man the black salt that I have created to protect his home, land, and family. Thank you for your protection of the land, this man, and his family. You were brave to help them. I know you wish to return to the woods and your ancestors. You are free to go. If you require me, just send a message into the white light, and I will come."

"Yes, we know. Thank you for the work you do for the Great Spirit," The leader said, and they melted back into the woods.

I could sense a small portal near the edge of the woods where they disappeared. It would be unwise to leave the portal open, so I closed it.

Turning back to the others, I smiled at them with a sense of relief.

"Well, are you going to tell us what happened?" Tina wanted to know. "We can't hear what you're saying in your head, so you'll need to give us the full rundown on it."

I told them what happened with the elemental and the Native Americans. Giving Tom the bag of black salt that I brought with me, I told him that he needed to lay down the salt right away.

"What you need to do is lay down a thin line of the salt. Lay it completely around the inside of your property. As you spread it, you're going to say, "in the name of Jesus Christ and God Almighty, I ask that nothing negative in this world or the next to be allowed to pass through this line of protection." This will keep anything negative from entering your property. You can also save a little bit from carrying on you and in your car to help extend that protection. I want to remind you that this will not keep out the good spirits, only the negative ones. You may have some that wander in from time to time, so you need to tell them that they are not allowed to stay," I instructed him.

"I do have a question about the black salt. What if it rains after or while I am laying down the salt? Will it still work?" Tom asked.

"Yes, it is still protecting you; if it rains, then the protection is taken into the land, and it's even better. The weather has no bearing on the laying down of the salt

"Let's say a prayer now to seal this protection," Stuart said. "Everyone hold hands, and we'll begin. Heavenly Father, I thank you for bringing us together to help this man in his hour of need. We ask that your blessing is upon our families and us in all we do. In the name of Jesus Christ, our Lord, amen."

"Thank you all so much for your help. I appreciate it and don't know what I would've done without it," Tom said, hugging each of us.

"If you ever need to talk or need anything, don't hesitate to call. Here's my number," Stuart said, handing Tom one of his cards for our paranormal group.

"If you have any questions or need my help again, don't hesitate to contact me. Remember, you may have the occasional good soul needing help to move on. Part of the price I ask of you for removing the demon is for you to help these souls go to the light. All you must do is tell them to look for the light and walk into it. There they will find their loved ones."

"I promise I'll help them if they come to me," Tom promised me.

"Thank you! I will talk to my wife, and I'll let you know. I appreciate your coming," he said, hugging me again. Getting in our cars, Stuart, Tina, and I headed back towards our homes.

About a week later, I received a text from Tom, letting me know that he felt more at peace than he had felt in a long time. He said that his home was now quiet and peaceful except for an occasional soul asking for help moving on. He told me that he had a dream about his wife, and she was laughing in the dream. He said it was the first time he'd had any communication from her since she had died two years earlier. He thanked me again for helping him.

PERCEPTION

There are varying descriptions regarding the appearance of beings of light and dark. No two people will see these beings in the same way. The reason behind this is quite simple. Everyone has their preconceived idea of what an angel or a demon should look like. No two people will have the same image in their heads. I have placed a few of the most common descriptions below.

The appearance of Dark Beings:
- Half man, half goat with horns.
- Human form with horns.
- Black mass, cloud, mist.
- Winged creature resembling a black angel.
- Black humanoid with glowing red or gold eyes.
- A human figure who is tall and thin wearing a hat.
- Cloaked grim reaper-like creature.
- Black spider-like creatures, snake-like creatures with big eyes.
- Black dog or cat.
- Low energy manifestation- red orbs.

Appearance of Light Beings:
- Angel with wings.
- Small chubby cupid-like angel.
- A human figure dressed as a warrior or in robes.

- A being of solid light too bright to look at.
- Shooting beams of light.
- Low energy manifestation- white or blue orbs.

All of these images are correct in how we, as humans, perceive them. Most people do not understand that they do not see the actual entity. You see an image that these beings project into your mind. Humans do not see negatives in their true form unless they have an angel residing within them. Their true image would be exceedingly difficult for most human minds to comprehend as it comprises a complex form of energy.

With demons, they will search the deepest recesses of your mind, in the place where your fears and nightmares exist. Once they find the images, they will magnify them image tenfold. The image elicits fear, terror, and anxiety in the individual. These negative emotions feed and energize the entities.

Negatives enjoy tormenting the living and may even take on the appearance of something harmless like a child, loved one, or animal to gain your trust. Once they have gained your acceptance and trust, they will try to get you to do things you would not ordinarily do. They start with little things that seem harmless enough. Then they move on to bigger things until, before you know it, you are under demonic oppression or influence.

Angels also pull out your image of them and make you see them as your preconceived images of angels, saints, or the Virgin Mary. It all depends upon your belief system. Only those angels reborn in human form can understand and process the true image.

Their goal is to comfort, reassure, and ally your fears, pain, and depression. The world would be an awful place without the thought of their comforting presence. We need the belief that good (the light) vanquishes all evil and that we are not alone in our hour of need. People need to understand that God does hear your prayers, and he has sent angels into the physical world to fight the negative entities. You might not see, hear or feel them, but they are never far when needed.

Thousands of warrior angels have been reborn in human form at this very moment. They are walking through the world quietly, protecting, bringing awareness, and creating a network of lightworkers to bring light to every corner of the world.

Eight archangels have been reborn into human bodies to walk among the living seeking out dark portals, demons, and people being terrorized by negative entities.

Most people would never know they were in the presence of a reborn angel, even if one was standing right in front of them. Even the demons have no idea that an archangel resides in the physical form. Like many people, Demons tend to look only on the surface, never looking any deeper, which is their undoing. Once the archangel surfaces, it is too late for the demon to escape.

SPIRIT ATTACHMENTS

What is an attachment, and why does it happen? An 'attachment' is when an entity, whether good or bad, which attaches itself to a person, place, or thing. Sometimes, the entity will interact with the conscious or subconscious person.

There are two types of attachments:

- A human spirit (a human soul, including animals)
- A negative entity (inhuman)

A human attachment occurs when a living person dies, and the soul stays earthbound (present on the earthly plane of existence, which we call a ghost). It's kind of like having an uninvited and unwanted house guest. Most of the time, you may have an unsettled feeling, feeling like something is in your vicinity, or you may feel like you are being watched. If the human spirit is negative, it can cause a lot of chaos in your life but is easily gotten rid of.

A human attachment may occur for several reasons. Here are just a few of the most common reasons:

- You resemble someone they used to know.
- They are a family member.
- You may have certain vices that you and the spirit share, substance abuse, gambling, or partying.

- The spirit may be a loved one who has not crossed over because it is waiting for a person to cross into the light to be together.
- The soul may only be looking for help to resolve their unfinished business, i.e., resolving a crime, a hidden document or treasure, etc.
- The spirit may not know it is dead-sometimes, the soul goes into shock like a human, and it wakes to find itself alone. It takes a while to realize that no one can see or hear them.
- You may have simply been in the right place at the wrong time.
- Sometimes the spirit may have a fear of judgment by God for some of the things it did in life.
- Sometimes it's a case of the spirit needing your energy so that it can do more in the physical world.

Any way you look at it, an attachment is never a good thing. Spirits should cross into the light and enter the heavenly realm. If the attachment is a human spirit, it can be easily helped. All you need to do is to sit down and talk to it. Let them know you are aware of them and try to help them. Let them know that they will find their loved ones in the heavenly realm. You should tell them to look for bright white light.

Once they see the light, they should go towards it and see their loved ones. Sometimes, the human spirit may not want to cross, but you can let them know that when they are ready, you will help them.

It's a whole other can of worms if you have an inhuman (aka negative entity, the dark one, demon) attached to you. These entities only want to cause harm and make your life a living hell. They have no intention of letting go of the person to whom they have attached themselves. The dark ones are always looking for easy prey. They search for people who have substance abuse issues, mental illness, are in an abusive situation, or have been traumatized by abuse. Emotionally unstable people have depression, and these entities easily manipulate anger issues. They also seek out people lacking in self-worth or who have been beaten down all of their life. All of these things make the person an easy target.

> **Effects of human spirit attachment:**

- Fatigue.
- Emotionally draining.
- You may experience feelings that are not your own.
- Vivid dreams are realistic and unsettling.
- You may become obsessed with a person, place, or thing.

> **Effects of negative entity attachments:**

- Nightmares.
- Intense run of bad luck, or it feels as if you have a dark cloud hanging over you.
- Paranormal activity is happening around you.
- Dark thoughts- suicide, harming another person, or animal abuse.

- You may experience depression, anger, jealousy, anxiety, paranoia, and radical mood swings.
- You may want to push everyone and everything you care about away from you- (negatives want to isolate you).
- Physical manifestations such as scratches, bite marks, welts, burns, and bruises appear on your skin out of nowhere. Words or symbols scratched into your skin, objects being moved or thrown, hearing voices.

POSSESSION

Possession is another form of spirit or inhuman attachment. It occurs when the negative entity takes control of your thoughts, body, and emotions. It is far more dangerous than a human spirit attachment and not as prevalent. Some of the more subtle physical changes that can happen are:

- Eyes can change in color, i.e., turning black, deepening in color. Increased strength, lack of physical sensation, i.e., pain due to injury.

- Mannerisms and behavioral changes to include increased anger, hostility, depression, and jealousy. Major personality changes, i.e., taking dangerous risks like driving recklessly or too fast.

- Cravings for alcohol, drugs, tobacco, even foods such as increased sugar and junk foods are completely out of character to the person's normal behaviors. They can turn someone to pornography and more addictive behavior

There are different degrees of possession:

Infestation: footsteps, voices, apparitions, furniture, or other objects are moving without human intervention, odors with no discernible source. Rather than directly affecting people, infestations affect property, objects, or even animals.

Oppression: physical attacks, regular nightmares, frequent and severe illnesses, major depression or anxiety, severe financial or employment problems, and relationship troubles. While these things happen in the ordinary course of life, all of them happening at once or in rapid succession could signify demonic presence.

Obsession: The afflicted person will have difficulty functioning and are always preoccupied with thoughts of the demonic activity taking over their life. They will become obsessed with thoughts of suicide. Sleep becomes almost impossible.

Partial possession is when the demonic will possess the person's body and mind sporadically. The person's consciousness is pushed to the back, and the demon takes possession. The person can see what's happening but is powerless to stop it.

Full possession is when a demon (or demons) takes full possession of the person's body and mind. The person is entirely unaware of what is happening.

If you should come across anyone with any of the above symptoms, the only thing you can do is seek help for them. This help must be a member of the clergy or a deliverance minister, or a demonologist. If one of these people should fail to help, you can seek out someone like myself. If you have been affected by demonic possession, infestation, or influence, the dark ones know who you are. They know because the person's physical body, mind, and spirit retain minute traces of dark energy. Once the removal is completed, you must be cleansed by bringing divine white light energy into yourself to push out any traces of the negative energy.

I contacted my para partner Wendy and my friend Stuart, an ordained minister, to see if they would like to accompany me on the removal. They both were interested in the case. I knew that both of them could use the experience in dealing with a possession case. "Make sure you both prepare; you will need all your strength and faith," I warned them.

Arriving at the location, I parked the car. The woman had some form of mental illness, but nothing would cause these manifestations. We joined hands and sent up a prayer for protection and guidance.

It took a few minutes before the door opened. The woman standing before us was disheveled, her hair hanging around her face. Her eyes were black, and the look on her face was one of pure evil. Her voice sounded deep and guttural as she said, "Get out; you don't belong here!" in the next moment, her face and eyes cleared. "Please come in."

I knew that for a minute or two, the woman had possession of her mind and not the demons. I used this to my advantage to help her understand what was going to happen. It took over three hours to complete the removal. I called the client the following week to see how she was doing. She told me she had started counseling for her PTSD and knew it would be an ongoing process, but she was relieved to be free of the entities.

A Case of Possession

I started doing podcasts in 2014 to promote my books, and in October 2017, I landed a spot on the show Ground Zero with Clyde Lewis. It is a very popular show with thousands of listeners. Once Clyde Lewis found out what I do, he was excited to get me on his show. He wanted to do a 4-hour special on me and what I do. There was a lot of interest in my appearance on the show. During the show, people were calling from all over the United States to talk to me and ask questions.

During the show, I spoke on several key points:

- What a negative entity is,
- how negatives think
- How to tell the difference between a demon from an earthbound spirit
- How to protect yourself
- Why do demons choose the individual?
- What are their goals are?

I received over two-hundred requests for help with demonic attachments in the days following the show. I continued to receive requests for help over the next several months. It took me months to do all the removals and answer the email questions.

I founded Ghosts and Girls Paranormal, specializing in negative entity identification and removal. I have a friend named Wendy who wanted to work with me to learn about negative entities. She is my para-partner and the sole member of my group. Although she cannot remove any full-blown demons, she can help with the little creepy crawly guys. She also is a lot more diplomatic than Auriel was in those days.

I received an email that stood out from a woman who said she was suffering from several attachments and possible possession. I let her know that I would help her. I asked her to send me a picture of herself. A couple of days later, I received a picture of her, and I could see multiple entities, some attached and some in possession.

I heard God say that I needed to take Wendy and Stuart with me to help the woman. Stuart is an ordained minister. *"You need to contact Stuart. He has a great fear of the dark ones and needs something to restore his faith in himself. This will provide the perfect challenge for him. It will not only test his faith but restore it as well. It will also strengthen Wendy's faith in me and in what you can do."*

I contacted Wendy to see if she could go with me to the removal.

"Hey girl, what are you doing this Saturday? I have a removal, and it's a very challenging one. are you up for a challenging removal this weekend?" I asked her.

"Sure, why not?" she responded.

"This is something you haven't encountered before. It is a possession with more than one entity. You've never encountered anything remotely like this. It will be a really taxing experience, and there is no room for doubt, or it could end badly. This is one of those cases that will make or break you. Your faith in yourself and God has to be absolute. I need to know for certain that you're strong enough to do this with me. If not, I need to know it now." I warned her.

"I understand; I believe that my faith in God is absolute and that he will guide and keep me safe from all harm. I know I'll have to prepare for it, a lot of prayers, a lot of talking with God and Jesus."

"If at any time you feel you cannot do this, then let me know. I won't think anything less of you." I assured her.

"No, I want to do this, I believe this is a test of faith for me, and I will not fail." She told me stanchly.

"Make sure you prepare; you will need all your strength and faith," I warned her.

"It sounds like we could use some heavenly help as well." She commented.

"Of course, always. I am going to ask Stuart to come along. He needs this experience to help strengthen his faith in himself. We have to be there around eleven. We'll meet at my house, and we'll go from there.

My next phone call was to Stuart. Picking up the phone, I dialed his number. It rang several times before he picked up.

"Stuart, what are you doing this coming Saturday?" I asked.

"I don't think I have anything planned; what's up?"

"Remember how you're always asking to go along on removals with me? Well, here is your chance to go with me and participate in a removal."

"Sure, I'd love to come. What time and where?" he asked.

"Be at my house at 10:30 on Saturday."

"Alright, with my collar or without?" He asked.

"Your collar and your entire kit. Make sure you prepare for what's to come. It's not going to be a walk in the park!" I warned him. "God told me you needed to come. He said, 'He needs to get over his fear of the dark ones if he's to help people.'"

"He's absolutely right; it's time I faced my fears; thank you for inviting me." He said seriously.

"You may not be thanking me by the time this is over," I warned him grimly.

Saturday dawned rainy and overcast, which suited my mood that morning. I spent a few hours preparing for the encounter with prayer and talking with the legion.

"You need to be aware that this removal is nothing like you've ever been on. There are multiple negatives attached to the woman.

There is possession involved, and although Auriel had been through these many times, it will be a new experience for not only you but Wendy and Stuart as well." Michael the archangel warned me.

"It will be a test of courage and faith for all of you. Stuart, if he succeeds, will gain a renewal of his faith and inner strength to face what lies ahead. Wendy will face her deepest fear. Both will have a newfound respect for the strength of negatives as well as Jesus." Gabriel assured me.

"Auriel will find that the human body she inhabits is not a hindrance and that you are stronger than she thinks." Raphael intoned.

Auriel knew they would be there for her when she needed them as they always had been. She was just too pigheaded to ask for help; she saw it as a weakness. It wasn't until she understood that their love and devotion to each other were stronger than any negative entity, even Lucifer.

Wendy and Stuart arrived at 10:30, and we left in my car and headed towards our appointment. Everyone was quiet for the short time it took to get to our client's apartment. We were all preparing in our own way to meet head-on what was coming. I had warned them that it would not be easy, but they didn't know just how many negatives, but I did.

From the moment I left my property, I could feel a strong presence of the negative entities. The closer we got to the client's apartment complex, the stronger presence of negative entities. I knew the woman had several attached to her; the negative energy was so strong it was almost overwhelming.

Parking, we joined hands and sent up a prayer for protection and guidance. "I just want to let you know that if at any time you feel your fate slipping away or feel you just can't make it through the removals, go outside. I would rather have you away from the situation than have the possibility of one of these negatives attaching or possessing you."

"I think we're ready; together, we can do this. This is going to be a test of our faith; one we must not fail." Stuart said, looking at Wendy for acknowledgment.

"He's right; I think this is something we all have to face. I think once we do, we'll be all the stronger for it." Wendy agreed.

"Alright then, are we ready to go?" I asked them.

"I'm ready," Wendy said.

"Yes, let's do it," Stuart said.

I led the way upstairs to the apartment; knocking on the door, we waited for her to answer.

"June, how many of them are there? Stuart asked. I feel like I'm surrounded."

"Yeah, it feels so heavy, I can hardly breathe." Wendy agreed.

It took a while for the door to be answered, and when she opened the door, I noticed her eyes were black, and the look on her face was one of pure evil.

Her voice was deep and guttural as she said, "Get out; you don't belong here!" in the next moment, her face and eyes cleared. "Please come inside."

As we entered the apartment, I could see eight entities staring at me and screaming.

"Get out b**** she is ours; you cannot have her. Stupid humans, you have no concept of what we can do to you. We will kill you and everyone else here." One of the nastiest ones said.

"We will kill the priest first and then the small woman; we will save you for last." Another large nasty one stated from somewhere within the woman.

"Thank God you've come; since you called, the activity has been a hundred times worse than it's ever been."

"I did warn you it would ramp up after you contacted me." I reminded her. "I want you to meet my friend Stuart; he's an ordained minister, and my friend Wendy, we work together doing removals. This is Cheryl, and she's had problems for a long time with demonic attachments."

"Thank you so much for coming, all of you. I don't know what I would have done. This has been going on for 20 years with no end in sight. I've tried to find help over the years, but no one would help me. I know these things are evil; they keep telling me to kill myself. They keep telling me that no one can help, that God and Jesus have deserted me. I know it's not true, but they keep trying to turn me against God."

"God has heard your prayer and has connected you with us to give you the help you were seeking. We will remove these entities from you. It will not be easy; they will fight me and try to kill you in the process. Are you ready to be rid of them?

I will not let that happen; it's time for them to go back where they came from. I'll have you sit in this chair; you must invoke the name of Jesus Christ and God."

"Stuart, I want you to grab a chair and sit in front of Cheryl where she can see you. I want everyone to start praying. Everyone must continue to pray. No matter what you see or hear, keep praying."

I closed my eyes, bringing Auriel forward. Once she came forward, I could see the negative entities within the woman. There were a total of 11 entities that needed to be removed.

Stuart had been praying since we arrived. Once Auriel came forward, Wendy and Stuart could hear growls. Something must have alerted Stuart because he turned to look at Cheryl's face and then turned white.

"Uh June, her eyes just turned black, and it wasn't her looking at me." He said nervously.

As Auriel's consciousness remained in control, it was she who responded.

"It is one of the eleven who reside within the body of this woman. I will remove them all." Auriel informed him.

The old demon who was the group leader spoke up, "Auriel, why are you residing in the body of this human female? You do not belong here; you have no authority over us."

"Who are you to say I have no authority over you? I am an archangel, a warrior for God, and as an archangel, I have authority over all things, including you. You are not supposed to be in the human world, and for that, you shall be punished." Auriel responded.

"We have just as much right here as you do. We will not let you tell us what to do. Lucifer has said we are free to do as we wish." The demon screeched back.

"Even Lucifer has limits on what he will let you do; I know this for a fact. E***** we have battled before, and you have lost. Are you ready to take that chance again? This time there will be no return to darkness; you will die here, over a human which you consider not worthy of you."

"I will not die; it will be you who will lose the battle and die." E***** shouted in response.

"So be it; I will not be merciful," Auriel warned him.

One by one, the demons came out of the woman attempting to attack the living. As each demon came forward, Auriel fought with it, slicing through it with her white light swords, effectively killing it.

Wendy and Stuart could only watch as the demons came out of the woman, and Auriel fought a silent battle against the demons. The battle seemed to last what felt like an eternity.

Once the external demons were defeated, Auriel turned to the ones possessing the woman's body. "Stuart, Wendy, I want you to pray as you never have before; her life depends upon it. I'm about to start the removal of the ones possessing her body." Auriel told them.

Stuart got up from his chair and pulled out his holy water, anointing oil, and crucifix. He then began to do a blessing on the woman using these items.

"So, it begins!" Auriel said with conviction and began the removal process.

The first ten entities were removed with a minimum of effort. Auriel felt an almost overwhelming sense of desperation from the remaining demon. It was almost as if it had more to lose than its hold on the woman, which was strange to her. Probing deep into the mind of the demon, she found out why there was this sense of desperation behind its possession.

"It's hiding from Lucifer." Auriel began to speak aloud so the others could hear at least one side of the conversation. "It seems the demon was given the assignment to do for Lucifer, and he decided not to do it. It is hiding out inside this woman to keep from being detected by Lucifer. It seems that if Lucifer finds him, death will be more merciful than what Lucifer has planned for him."

The demon came forward, and Auriel turned her attention to the demon. She made sure it knew that she was aware of its dilemma.

"I understand that you were supposed to do a job for lucifer and did not do it. Lucifer does not give assignments out for no reason, and failure to do the job is not an option. If you do not want to return to the darkness and wish to return to the light, I will ask Jesus to take you home. Jesus come forth. I have a demon who may wish to return to the light. Will you help?"

Jesus's hand and arm appeared out of nowhere. He stretched out his hand toward the demon. I noticed Stuart and Wendy step aside as a large outstretched arm and hand came toward the woman.

"He has come for you, demon; you have only to reach out and take his hand if you wish to go home," Auriel told the demon.

Auriel could see the demon being tempted to take what was offered.

"I can go home, even after all I've done?" it asked.

"If you truly want to go home, he will take you home. However, you will have to answer for your crimes," Auriel responded.

"No, no, you're lying; I don't trust you! I won't leave this human; why should I? Lucifer will never find me." It screeched at Auriel.

Jesus withdrew his hand, and the demon settled back into the woman.

"Stupid demon, you don't know when you are well off. Auriel warned it. Now you will pay the price for your stupidity."

"You will never get me to leave the human; she will suffer for the rest of her life." The demon laughed.

"So be it; you have sealed your fate. I tried to help you when all I wanted to do in the first place was to kill you. You would have been better off being dead; Lucifer will deal with you." Auriel told it, smiling in delight at the fate she knew would await it.

"He'll never find me; he hasn't a clue as to where I am!" The demon laughed evilly.

"Oh, he'll find you; I promise you that because I'll tell him! Lucifer, I command you, come forth!" Auriel said, summoning Lucifer.

A black humanoid figure in a 1920's style suit appeared at the end of the hall in plain sight of everyone. I glanced at Wendy and Stuart to find their expressions mirrored shock, dismay, and awe. As Lucifer moved towards her, Auriel bowed. She bowed not indifference to him but his position and the respect owed him.

"Here is the renegade demon you seek. It has been hiding in this woman; that is why you have been unable to find him." Auriel informed him.

"S****** remove yourself from this human; you have much to answer for," Lucifer commanded the demon.

"No, I will not leave!" The demon screamed at Lucifer.

Lucifer turned and looked at Auriel. "If I remove it at this moment, it will kill the woman, and I know that is not acceptable to you. I will return for it tonight, and I will not be nice about it." Turning to glance at the demon inside of the woman Lucifer said menacingly. "I will return for you; you can be sure of that!" He turned and walked back down the hallway disappearing.

Auriel receded, and my consciousness came forward. I moved to stand in front of Cheryl. "I've done all I can; ten of them have been removed. There is one left inside of you, which Lucifer will return for tonight."

"Oh, okay, I do feel lighter, but you're right; I can still feel it inside me," Cheryl said.

"I want you to find a mental health provider and get some counseling. You're suffering from PTSD after living with these things inside of you for twenty years." I told her. "Let's keep in touch; let me know how it goes for you," I told her, hugging her.

We said our goodbyes and headed to the car. Once in the car, I heard Stuart and Wendy expel a collective breath.

"Words fail me; I still cannot wrap my head around what just happened," Stuart said. "Did I just see Lucifer and Jesus in the same place? I mean, when you summoned Lucifer for just a split second, I thought you had taken leave of your senses. Then I remembered who and what you are, and I wasn't afraid."

"I'm still in awe at being in God's presence and the overwhelming presence of Lucifer. It's going to take me a while to process everything that's happened, and even then, I'm not sure if anyone would believe me." Wendy said in a dazed voice.

"I'll bet you never knew I moved in such exalted company!" I teased them, laughing.

"You know, all my life, I've known God has been there; I could always sense him. But today, I got absolute confirmation of him being real.

As for Lucifer, it hurt my eyes to look at his face, and the feeling of intense evil made me want to throw up." Stuart said, still feeling a sense of awe.

It surprised me that two and a half hours had gone by. Auriel has never been out for that long before, and it's never taken her so long to remove the demons. But then, she's never had to deal with eleven demons in the physical world at one time. All of which were in possession of the person."

"How will we know when Lucifer has removed the last demon?" Wendy asked.

"Oh, I'll know, but I'm not sure if you'll know until I tell you, although you may," I said consideringly.

Later that night, all three of us woke up in our respective beds at 3 a.m. to Lucifer, saying, "It is done."

I contacted Cheryl the next day, and she told me she finally felt free of the demonic presence.

PROTECTION

Light beings can help guide and protect us in life with their thoughts. Our loved ones want what is best for us but are not powerful enough to protect us from dark entities. Knowing this brought the reality of how dangerous this could be for the living and how vulnerable we humans are. Each physical body contains a white light being, and we are most vulnerable while we are in physical form.

One important piece of information I brought back with me when I died and went to the other side was that thought becomes a reality in the heavenly and dark realms of existence. It is the intention behind the thought that gives it power. There is no distance, unlike here, where you must drive or fly to get somewhere. This is how the archangels can be in a thousand places simultaneously. If you think of Disneyland, you are instantly transported there. This has proved to be a useful tool against dark entities.

Therefore, I consider this chapter one of the most important chapters within this book. Attention to detail must be taken when reading this chapter. I can hear and see what most others cannot. I know beyond the physical world, moving and walking amongst us. Our loved ones are always close by, protecting and helping us. However, with light, there is dark, and it is these dark entities that we need to protect ourselves and others from.

Since the advent of humanity, people have tried all manner of things to protect themselves from 'evil spirits.' These have ranged from herbs, trees, stones, crystals, and even symbols. Some of these tools, such as yoga and meditation, can increase the energy flow to the body mind and elevate the spirit. Both are tools that help ground and detox the negative energy which we all carry with us. Centering yourself with prayers and meditation can help to strengthen your faith.

The stressors of work, school, and family can cause depression, anger, irritability, and anxiety, all forms of negative energy. Negative entities thrive on this type of energy and will use it to create an atmosphere of discord and chaos. Negative energy empowers, strengthens, and feeds these entities, and if there is no negativity or chaos, they will create it.

It is not just humans who attract these entities; they can also be attracted to buildings, land, bodies of water, or an object.

Buildings- because it has seen death violence, the people in the building are abusive, negative, or prime targets. They will draw energy from the people who work or reside in the building.

Land- has seen death, violence, the presence of quartz or bedrock is situated on or near a ley line.

Water itself conducts electromagnetic energy, which attracts spirits and negatives.

Objects- can and do hold energy from people, events, spirits, angelic beings, and negative entities. Quartz is known to hold energy for years; it's like a sponge soaking up the energy. It can act like a tape recorder, recording events through the energy and playing them back at random times or when activated by another event.

Things That Will Not Protect You

There is a lot of misinformation about what will and what won't protect you from negative entities. Here are a few of the myths:

Break dust- laid down in entryways is an old wives' tale, and I have never seen it work as a barrier or protection.

Tar water or (War Water), also known as "**Oil of Tar** in water (filtered)" Oil of Tar is a thick distillate of creosote or burned pine resin (sometimes called Pine Tar), and it is carcinogenic and dangerous. This old medicine mixture is rarely used anymore because of the dangers of making and using it.

Crystals- can be used to amplify the energy surrounding or placed into them.

Talismans, amulets, and figurines- can attract good energies as well as negative energies.

Paintings or Cards with a rendering of Christ will help you focus and connect with the light but will not provide active protection.

Eye of Horus or a **Pentagram-** hanging them over the entrance of your house is like an open for business sign and -may attract unwanted entities.

A Plain Cross- without an image of Christ or with an abstract image. This will not protect you because it is without meaning.

Ignoring the Entity will only cause the entity to escalate its activity.

Sage, Sage Candles, or **Incense**- the use of sage will only incite the negative entities. This is because they know you are aware of them and trying to get rid of them.

White Salt can protect a home from human entities (earthbound spirits) but will not protect against demonic entities.

Stones for Protection-Black tourmaline, amethyst, black obsidian, and fluorite are commonly used for protection. None of these will protect against inhuman entities. Can you explain the difference?

Metals, Pendants, or Coins with the images of a saint on them- Some believe that if you bury these in the four corners of your property, it will protect you against negative entities. They will help against negative human spirits but not inhuman entities. If they are blessed, it will help ward them off, but that is all.

Thinking positive thoughts or sending the negatives love and light is an exercise in futility. It distracts your mind from what is happening to you, making you vulnerable to their attack.

Not believing in them doesn't matter if you believe in them or not, because they believe in you. And that's all they need to cause you irreparable harm.

Controlling your negative emotions Yes, it's important to keep your negative emotions such as fear, anxiety, worry, and despair under control. These emotions feed the negatives and make them stronger.

Walking in a circle backward three times- is merely an old superstition and does not work.

Gargoyles or other grotesque faces-this was a first-line defense in medieval times but continues to be used in some cultures.

Knowing what I have learned about the dark side of its devastation on a person's mental, emotional, and physical health, I can understand and sympathize with why people are afraid and will try anything to protect and rid themselves of negative entities. The items listed above are just a few of the items people have used to protect themselves, and they have failed.

I genuinely wish I could tell you these things work for protection against negative entities, but unfortunately, they do not. I know this from 40 years of experience and what I have learned from many conversations with archangels. I have spent the last forty years helping others break free of these negative entities.

I have spoken and worked with people with negative entity attachments for several years. Most of these people have no one to turn to, no knowledge of how to help themselves, and are afraid to say anything because they don't want anyone to think they are crazy. They are so desperate for help that they will literally try anything to get rid of the entity, no matter how outlandish it sounds.

To find help, they look for someone to help them locally, like a shaman, psychic, or minister. Having failed to find anyone to help them or what someone recommends fails to work, they will turn to the internet to seek help.

Some of the things people have tried are:

- **Take coffee or salt baths.**
- **Walking backward in a circle three times.**
- **Sleeping with tobacco under your pillow.**

- **Yelling at the entity.**
- **Singing religious songs.**
- **Carrying a silver or iron coin.**
- **Eating garlic or ginseng.**
- **Positive thoughts Positive energy.**
- **Sending the entity love and light**
- **White magic.**
- **Tying a black ribbon or string around their wrist and ankle.**

You may think these things are funny, stupid, or ridiculous, but I can assure you that your life is a living hell when you have a negative entity attached to you.

Negatives will begin by isolating you from your family and friends, your financial, mental, and physical health will deteriorate. You will be plagued by what seems like a run of bad luck, i.e., losing your job, car accident, breach in your financial accounts, just to name a few things that have happened to people. Some people have been suffering for years, so you can see why the person is driven to the point of desperation and is willing to try *anything* to get rid of the entity.

Unfortunately, when portals are left, unwelcome open spirits or negative entities can make their way into the physical world. The dark entities delight in creating chaos and causing destruction to your physical health, mental health, finances, and relationships. This is when your life suddenly starts spiraling downwards.

They can and do put thoughts into your mind. They will influence you to do things you would not normally do, such as commit suicide physically hurt someone or an animal. You might hear voices growls; things may be thrown, moved, or you may be physically attacked. You might think you are losing your mind.

Many people have come to me who have suffered because of negative entities and unwanted spirits over the years. Most people who come to me have never used anything to open a portal. They may have either unknowingly visited a haunted location or simply have been in the wrong place at the right time. I have even had quite a few paranormal investigators who have unknowingly brought entities home with them. These people's lives are thrown into turmoil, their problems start to escalate, and soon they are at the end of their rope.

They feel powerless to help themselves, not knowing who and where to turn to. They are plagued with anxiety, illness, 'bad luck,' nightmares, and physical attacks by the entity. You are at your most vulnerable during sleep because your mind is open, and the negatives can reach in and give you terrible nightmares and subconsciously influence you.

Your house is no longer a place of peace and sanctuary. The house begins to fill with negative energy, and you constantly feel like you are not alone, as if someone is watching you.

When someone contacts me, they are stressed, desperate, and have almost lost all hope. Several people have told me that they read my book The Dark Side of the Paranormal, and it helped them understand what was happening to them. It was then that they decided to seek my help. One man explained that he had been having difficulties at home and work for a couple of years. He has abilities and can sense the negatives around him but does not know how to help himself.

The negatives had created a portal, which had been opened in the building where he had his business. He told me he had contacted other people for help, none of which could help him. He was advised to use white salt, crystals, sage, tobacco, salt baths, and even a ritual of walking backward in a circle three times.

These things may sound amusing, but when you are suffering a constant barrage of demonic attacks, not sleeping because you are either having horrible nightmares or being assaulted, you are desperate for help. He was being physically assaulted in his home, especially while sleeping; he would wake up with scratches and bruises all over him. His elderly mother didn't understand what was happening to him; she thought he had problems at work. She thought he was overreacting until she saw an arm with claws come through the house wall and reach out for her. His business began to fail, and his staff was leaving because of the negative activity in the building.

When he contacted me, it was clear this man was desperate for help. He had even spoken to me about ending his life. I worked closely with him to clear out the negatives. His business picked up once the negatives were removed, and his mental and physical health improved. The man is now at his new premises, and we talk often.

One investigation I was called into is an excellent example of the need for protection and how negatives will attack even a Minister. The minister is a friend of mine named Stuart. With this, I would like to highlight even those who have a strong belief in God are not immune. The investigation took place at the Norblad Hotel in Astoria, Oregon.

Part of the paranormal investigating team had just come out of the hotel's basement. I could see by Stuart's face that something was wrong. Stuart explained that a negative entity had just attacked him. He said he saw a dark shadow move by him, and he felt something grab his spine, giving him unbearable pain. This lasted the whole time he was in the basement and did not ease until he was back outside. He said he forgot to put his protection in place as he was late getting to the location.

Negatives focus on a person's weakness, be it physical or mental, and will use that to cause harm to them. Stuart has a spinal disease, which was where the demon attacked him.

Luckily, I was there and could stop it, but this could easily have been anyone. The dark ones are dangerous, and they are relentless in causing pain and suffering to the living.

Therefore, any time you communicate with the spirit realm, whether it is using Tarot cards, a pendulum, or your mediumistic abilities, you must make sure you have your protection in place. There is always the chance of encountering someone or something negative in nature. Just because you intend to contact the white light souls does not mean this will happen.

It would be best if you were proactive in protecting yourself and the people around you. Each time you use a tool for divination, whether a pendulum, divining rods, tarot cards, playing cards, scrying, intuitive reading, or an Ouija board, you open a doorway to the other side. This should not be left open as negative spirits can abuse this and affect people in ways that I have described. Even when doing a paranormal investigation, there is always the chance of encountering a negative entity. Keeping this in mind, I have made a list of items that you can use for protection.

What Will Protect You

- **A crucifix with the image of Jesus. (a symbol related to your belief system)** It must be a physical likeness because there is power in his image.

- **Blessed Black salt**- I was given a recipe for the black salt by my guardian, who, in turn, received the instructions for creating it from the archangels. The recipe was dictated to me by God and blessed at each creation process step.

You can find it on my website: demonseer.com. Many people create black salt, but none of them have the ability to put divine energy into the mix and have it personally blessed by God. It has powerful protecting power.

- **Prayer invokes God and Jesus's name** (or whatever deity you have faith in). - this helps to keep the negatives at bay.

- **Holy water and the Blessed anointing oil**- can be used to bless objects people and seal windows and doors. You place a sign of the cross over the doors and windows of the building. While applying the water or oil, ask that nothing negative be allowed to cross into the home in the name of Jesus Christ and God. Before you sell the house, you must make certain there is nothing negative still within the building, or you will trap in inside with you.

- **Rosary-** It must be blessed and has the image of Jesus; it will ward off negativity.

- **Holy Relics**- such as a blessed metal, clergy vestments including stoles, and kippah (Jewish cap worn by the Rabbi)- have been blessed.

- **Summoning an archangel for protection**- you can summon an archangel by saying: "Through the blood of Jesus Christ, I summon Michael (angelic name) the archangel to defend me against this evil."

- **Statue of the Virgin Mary or Saints**- these statues alone will not protect you. They will help ward off negative entities if they are blessed but not completely remove them.

- **Pleading the blood of Christ**-"In the Name of Jesus, I plead the blood of Jesus over (the person, place, or thing).

- **White light protection**-The white light protection exercise at the end of this chapter can protect you against attacks by negative entities. Once you get proficient at it, you can create a ball of energy to send to someone in danger to surround and protect that person.

Without protection, you are leaving yourself vulnerable to negative entities who will be only too happy to guide you into destruction and make you feel like you are the one who is going insane.

There are thousands of paranormal investigation teams. Some teams are more conscientious than others about using protection. It should be up to the group's leader to ensure everyone knows what to use for protection and properly use it. It is up to the team's individual members to put their protection in place before they arrive at the location for the investigation.

Negative entities do not just attach to people; they may also attach themselves to items that belong to the person. If not all the members of the group use protection, it may adversely affect the other members of their team. It can also affect the person who owns, lives, or manages the location. I have had to help numerous investigators who did not use protection and have suffered consequences as a result.

One person reported that her car began to go wrong after a paranormal investigation in a house where there were known negative entities. She reported the leader did not use or encourage the team members to use protection. This happened when she first began investigating haunted locations. Her car was new; not long after the investigation, the dashboard lights in her car suddenly stopped working. The garage she took it to could not find the problem, and even the lights in the repair shop would flicker.

The garage installed a new part, and the car company stated that this was the first time this part had failed. The car was stolen and in a hit-and-run accident shortly after this. Luckily, no one was seriously hurt. With this in mind, before doing paranormal investigations or using any of the above tools, you need to ask for protection and blessing from whatever deity you believe in.

If you are doing an intuitive reading, ask for clarity and information needed for the person's greater good. Once you finish using the tools, doing the reading, or investigating, you must thank the deity for their blessing and ask them to close the portal.

Once a negative entity enters our world, it can do just about anything they want to. They can attach themselves to a person, building, object, or piece of land. The sole purpose of the negative entity is retribution against the white light soul inhabiting the physical body.

Many mediums believe in the use of crystals for protection. They believe that wearing the crystal in a necklace near the heart chakra will provide protection. Unfortunately, this is a fallacy; it offers no protection against negative entities because it only amplifies its energy.

Whenever you enter a location with known paranormal activity, you should have at least some form of basic protection in place, whether it is negative or not. This is because negative entities can and are attracted to locations with intense paranormal activity.

Here is a protection exercise that will create a white light force field. Before you begin the exercise, ask for God's protection and guidance. Why? Because any time you open yourself up, you are vulnerable to negative entities.

Find yourself in a comfortable position where you are unlikely to be disturbed. Take several slow deep breaths, paying attention to the movement of your breathing.

Once you are relaxed, focus your thoughts on creating an opening on the top of your head, and then see it open up.

You ask that any physical, spiritual, mental, or emotional negativity be released from you. You notice a white light coming down from God's realm and going directly into the opening at the crown of your head. As the light enters your body, it starts to fill it from the feet upward. As it fills your body, you notice all the negativity leaving you to be released among the stars.

As the light fills you, you notice a sense of absolute peace coming over you. You bask in the feeling as the light continues to fill you. Once the light has filled your body, it bubbles over your head surrounding your body in a white light force field, which can protect you from all negativity.

In time you learn to manipulate the field to expand outward or retract close to your body. As you become proficient in manipulating the field, you can even send it across thousands of miles to protect someone. I have done this on several occasions.

After doing this for a while, it will become second nature to you, and you will have it in place automatically; there will be no need to think about it.

DEATH

THE FINAL EXIT POINT

What is an exit point? An exit point is the moment the soul leaves the body. The soul knows its exit point, and if you have made the soul connection, you will have an instinctive knowledge of a general time but not the exact moment of your death. Does the soul know its moment of death? If it does know, are we able to tap into that knowledge? Is our death set in stone, or can we alter it?

Before we return to physical life, we decide what we want to experience. You may want to have a life where you experienced cancer, a father, a woman, childbirth, or mental illness. You are curious about what a life would be like with one of these issues. It's all fine and good watching someone else experience these issues, but you don't get the true meaning until you experience it yourself.

If we have been in the white light realm for an extended period, we may lose the connection with the physical consciousness, which includes feelings of pain, fear, joy, worry, and love. We remember the concept, but we do not remember what it feels like. Did you ever have someone walk up to you and say, "I know exactly what you're feeling?" When they haven't a clue what you are going through or how you feel. They can only imagine what it is like. It is like that for the soul who has been in the white light realm for too long.

It's like that for the soul; they can only imagine how you feel because they do not feel your pain, sorrow, or joy. They want to experience the individual life they are living to the fullest to get every moment of experience they can get out of that lifetime. It doesn't matter if it's pain, fear, love, joy, or worry.

When the soul plans its death, it doesn't think about the pain, suffering, fear, or people left behind. We are too focused on the experience of death itself. Only the soul and God know the exact moment of a physical body's death.

I think it's rather ironic that we know how we are going to die but not the circumstances surrounding the death, such as:

- Where the death takes place, i.e., at home, work, sitting on the toilet.
- Who is with us at the precise moment of death?
- What is happening in our surroundings at the moment of death, i.e., in a burning building, skiing, hiking, having sex.

Near-death experiences occur for one of two reasons:

- Give the person a wake-up call because their life is going in a bad direction.
- To reveal something very important, even life-changing.

Here is the story of how dying changed my life completely. In September 1987, I died in a motorcycle accident; I was clinically dead for 2 minutes; my experience follows.

Dead And Back Again

It was early Sunday morning, and I was watching cartoons. I love the old Looney Tunes with Wiley Coyote. Wiley was just about to get smashed when the screen disappeared. In its place, I was seeing through the eyes of a person riding a motorcycle. I could not see the type of bike-only the handlebars and the road ahead. The person on the bike was making a left-hand turn on a green light when I saw a flash in the mirror. A car was headed straight for me from the right and not stopping. I didn't see but felt the impact, then blackness, and the vision stopped.

I should have known that the warning was for me, but I misinterpreted the message. My two younger brothers and I rode motorcycles at that time. I assumed the warning was for my brothers as they are both reckless drivers. On the other hand, I have always been a very cautious rider. One week later, the vision became a reality.

The following week was busy at work. I worked in a doctor's office, seeing patients, and doing x-rays. I didn't have a chance to take my bike out until Saturday. It was a beautiful fall day, perfect for riding. I had just repossessed my older bike, a 1979 Suzuki GL 425. The bike sat up high off the ground and was built for speed.

I had repossessed the bike a week before, and I was going to teach Dan, the man I was dating, how to ride a motorcycle.

It was a perfect day for a ride, so I decided to take the bike out for a spin to ensure it was in good running condition. The ride was short but pleasant. I was on my way home when I decided to ride the bike out to Dan's house in Gresham at the last minute. I had two bikes at the time and would teach him on the bigger of the two. I decided this bike would be the one I would teach him on.

Coming to an intersection, I maneuvered into the left turn lane. The left turn light had just turned green, so I started through the intersection. Entering the intersection, I saw a flash of an oncoming car out of the corner of my eye. Turning my head, I had just enough time to see the oncoming vehicle. Instinct took over, and I remembered to push myself off the opposite side of the bike. I never made it completely off the bike before the impact.

I did manage to get my right leg over the seat before the car hit. The force of the impact sent me flying off the bike and across the road. My body landed about 100 feet from the crash site. I was not wearing a helmet, and I hit my head on impact. It was at that moment when I felt my soul leave my body.

A bright white light surrounded me, and it felt warm, welcoming, and loving. In the distance, I could see two people walking toward me. I ran toward them, hugging each of them tightly. As they drew closer, I could see my grandma and grandpa smiling at me.

"Grandma, grandpa, how can you be here? Am I dead?" I asked.

"You're here because your body just died," Grandma said.

"You're here for a reason." A voice said from behind them, and I instantly recognized Michael, the archangel's voice, as he stepped forward. "You need to understand who and what you are outside of this incarnation. It is why you are having this experience now. You need to start doing the work that you were meant to do in all your lifetimes."

At first, I didn't notice the figure standing behind my grandparents.

"What do you mean who I am? You know who I am, Michael," I responded in bewilderment.

"You're still thinking like a human." He admonished me. "Come here; I want to show you something."

Taking my hand, he led me a couple of steps to what looked like a bay window appeared. "Look down there." He instructed me.

Stepping closer, I peered through the window. The window looked down on the earth, and I could see every person who was alive at that moment. They all had what appeared to be threads coming out of their heads.

"Why are their threads connected to the people's heads?" I asked him.

"The threads you see are the connection to the soul. The threads that are alight are the people who have made the connection to their souls. The people with the darker threads have not made the connection yet." He explained.

"So, if this is heaven, what about hell? Does it exist?" I asked.

He turned around led me away from the window to a large open area. He stopped in an area that looked like a floor made of dense white clouds. He stretched out his arm, and the clouds parted. A black hole opened; I could hear terrible screams and saw hands reaching up out of what looked like black molasses. He waved his arm again, and the hole closed.

"Okay, that answered my question," I told him.

"It's time for you to understand who you are." He informed me and touched my forehead immediately; it was as if I were living lives at the speed of light. I could see, hear, feel, and experience these past lifetimes. As fast as the review began, it was over, and I suddenly became aware of separate consciousness. I was no longer in my physical body, and my appearance was similar to Michael's. I was as tall as Michael, and I thought, *I wish I had a mirror,* and suddenly one appeared in front of me. I was not startled, which seemed odd, then the awareness came to me. Looking in the mirror, I saw long, flowing dark auburn hair and bright blue-green eyes that were as light in color as to almost be white. In this world, thought becomes a reality.

"You are Auriel the Archangel, guardian of the throne of God, Demon Slayer, and Assassin of old. You have been sent back to relive mortal lives because you removed a demon from a woman, and she died. You felt no compassion or concern for the mortal woman. You had lost all care for mortals.

The human lives you have lived have taught you compassion for humanity. It's time you started doing the job you are well suited for in this lifetime; you are a demon slayer." Michael informed me.

"Is that why I seem to know things instinctively, like the fact that thought becomes a reality here?" I asked. "I also know it can also work in the physical world."

"Yes, there are many things you will know instinctively to be true when you return to your body. It is the intent behind the thought that gives it power. However, you will not be allowed to have full knowledge as you do now, but the information you need will be known to you."

"After all, you've got a long life ahead of you, another 65 years." My Grandpa interjected.

"How old is Auriel?" I asked curiously.

"It's hard to calculate in human years, but the closest I can come to it is a hundred and fifty billion of your years," Michael said somberly. "We are what you would call an ancient race. Now you must return to your body; you have much more work to do."

I thought for a moment, remembering my short life, and knew they were right. "I know you're right; I do need to return. There's so much more that I need to accomplish in this lifetime."

"You have a job to do for God, but that won't start for a while," Grandma informed me.

"You're going to have a son, June Ann, and I'll be there to watch over him for you," Grandpa told me, smiling.

"Wow, a son, I think I'll name him after you grandpa, Ray," I told him, smiling.

"Thank you, but it's time for you to return to your body." He said.

"How do I do that?"

"Think about returning to your body, and it will happen. If this were the end of your life, you wouldn't be able to return to your body."

I gave both my grandparents a big hug, then thought about returning to my body, and suddenly I was there lying on the pavement with a police officer standing over me. He seemed to be checking for a pulse. I was dead for less than two minutes, but it seemed like hours on the other side. When he noticed my eyes open, he let out a sigh of relief. "You're alive!" he told me, sounding as if he were trying to convince himself more than me.

At first, I had no memory of the actual accident because of a concussion, but eventually, I remembered the impact. For a year after the accident, I had short-term memory loss. It's funny, but the one thing that I didn't forget was my visit to the other side, seeing my grandparents and learning who I am. I never told anyone about dying until I decided to write my books.

It took me a good two years to come to terms with what I had inside me, to say nothing of the fact that I had been dead and returned. A little over a year after my accident, my son was born. After about of postpartum depression, I decided to finally come to terms with the angelic being inside of me.

I didn't even know there was an archangel named Auriel. I researched online to see what I could find out about Auriel. All I could find is that she was one of the five angels guarding the throne of God, and her name means lion of God. I decided if I was going to start removing demons, I needed more information on Auriel, and for that, I would need to be able to communicate with her.

I asked Michael if he would help, and he told me he could do a merge between the soul consciousness and the physical consciousness.

"You share a consciousness, and yet they are separate. You can consciously hear her thoughts when you try. When I do the merge, you will hear her thoughts at will and ask her questions. She will help teach you about her life and her abilities. She will enable you to create white light swords to kill demons. We will teach you how to create infinity orbs, close, and create portals. You will have a greater ability to see the future, heal, and other gifts you have barely tapped into." Michael informed me.

I have always been able to see negatives but did not have my first real interaction with one of them until I was nineteen. At that time, I did not know what lay within my physical body, but I think the demon knew because it left in a hurry.

ANGELIC CONNECTION

Since 1985, I noticed more negative entities around me but didn't do my first removal until 1984. After the first removal, my life changed in subtle ways at first. I started to use social media to get the word out about helping people with their paranormal issues. It was slow at first, and most of what I was getting were readings, house clearings, and blessings.

As my connection with Auriel grew stronger, my abilities grew exponentially. I started to be able to sense when something negative was coming months in advance. I could tell what type of negative it was, and I learned how to tell about when it would show up. I was doing fine with what I was doing, but no one was coming to me because they needed help with negatives.

Auriel and I needed to come to a meeting of the minds because she would come forward whenever she sensed a negative close by. She also had a very bad attitude concerning humans, which showed their disdain. I decided I needed to enlist Michael's help to make Auriel understand she couldn't have an attitude or come forward whenever she felt like it.

Michael suggested we talk to her together, so I went into a deep meditation to work things out our consciousnesses.

"You can't treat people with disdain even though you may have those feelings," I told her.

"Why not? It's how I feel?" She questioned earnestly. I could tell she was surprised at this information.

"Yes, I understand it's how you feel, but you need to remember I have to live in this physical world. If your attitude comes through, it will reflect on me. People will think it is my attitude because they can't see, feel, or hear me. They won't want to refer cases to me, and you won't get to do any removals."

I could see she was thinking seriously about what I had just said. After a moment, she said. "Alright, I have to learn to be more tolerant of these humans. If that's what it takes to be able to do removals in your world, I will do it." She agreed.

"Auriel, I know you don't wish to be here in the physical world, but you have to make the best of it. Remember, it's your lack of caring for the humans that got you here in the first place." Michael reminded her.

I could feel Auriel becoming frustrated with the limitations she was forced to endure. I started to speak to her each night to help her understand what it was like to be a human in the physical world. I would answer her questions, and she would answer mine. When we got to the part about emotions, she explained what it was like on the other side.

"You must understand, we archangels have not had physical form for billions of your years. Our problem is we cannot relate to your emotional issues. We understand the concept of love, hate, sorrow, and depression, but we do not understand the actual emotion. I decided it was time for the other archangels to feel these emotions to relate better to humans.

I leave your body at night and return to the angelic realm to catch up on what is happening there. Then, I share the emotions you are experiencing with the others. This way, they can understand what you are feeling. I believe this will bring us closer to understanding humanity." She told me.

"I agree. I think this will help all the archangels to understand why we do the things we do and be able to relate our emotional issues." I agreed with her.

From that time on, Auriel and I have had constant communication. We have our differences of opinions, but we always work it out.

SHADOW PEOPLE

Is there such thing as an entity known as a shadow person? Is it just an urban legend or a figment of our imagination? Were they once living, breathing people, or are they something darker, more sinister? Where do they come from, and why are they here? Can they hurt us, and if so, why would they want to? Why don't most people seem to know what they are and where they come from?

There are several theories about what or who they are, but no one has been able to say for certain just what they are.

- One theory is that they are demons and have never had a human existence.
- Others believe they are the negative part of a person's soul left behind after the person dies.
- The last theory is that they are ghosts like any other, except they are negative.

According to the archangels, each theory has a grain of truth. These shadowy creatures have never had human form, nor are they ever likely to, which makes them very unpredictable.

When God first encountered us as a primitive race in another galaxy, the dark ones were white light beings. That was billions of years ago before we evolved into pure energy.

As we all did in the beginning before we came to this planet, they had a physical form. They were the last to evolve because they still tended to hold on to their selfish ways.

We could not leave and travel the galaxies until the rest of our souls had evolved. We could not leave anyone behind, especially the last ones, to evolve because they might cause trouble.

You will find mention of the shadow creatures in many folk tales and legends from bygone years. Because of the advancement in communications in the last two hundred years, people are becoming more and more aware of these beings. They are not just scary tales anymore; they are real whether we like them or not.

Shadow people are very dangerous to both humans and earthbound spirits. They can strangle and choke the life out of a person. The very young animals and very old are particularly vulnerable to them. They can hold earthbound spirits and keep them from ascending into the light. They can suck the life force out of a person over a long period of time or all at once, depending on if they want to prolong the person's suffering.

These shadow entities enter our world using portals. These portals can and do occur anywhere and everywhere. A portal can be anywhere inside a home, business, barn, or outside in the woods, your yard, or even a cemetery. Humans cannot destroy shadow creatures, although we can banish them back into the dark realm.

If you have a shadow entity or suspect you have a shadow entity in your home, you can call on God to send an Archangel to do battle with it.

THE WAR BETWEEN
HEAVEN AND HELL

Our souls have consisted of pure complex energy for over a hundred and fifty thousand years. As a race, we prized knowledge and compassion above all things. Our goal is to acquire as much knowledge as possible, learn all that can be learned, and create a world without petty differences. We began to travel among the stars and observe the birth of heavenly bodies, new civilizations, and even the creation of galaxies. We wanted to create harmony among all the souls by bringing them together in a unified cause.

It worked to a certain extent, but as with all things, there are always those who still seek to be the center of everything, want to be first or in charge, or believe they are better than everyone else. Those who sought to put themselves above all others created tensions and dissension between the souls.

Everyone enjoyed traveling, learning, and observing the birth of galaxies, black holes, and new worlds. We traveled for what would be millions of years in our time. Some longed for physical love, children, and experiencing all the physical and emotional sensations of life. Gradually there began a movement to return to a physical body.

When they voiced their opinions, some didn't want to be a part of it. They did not want to be subject to existing in a physical shell, unable to travel the galaxies if they so chose. They were unwilling to experience birth, death, pain, disease, and suffering.

This dissension gave way to an all-out war between those who wanted to be physical and those who did not. Lucifer led the opposing forces against God, Jesus, and the heavenly Legion. He felt they were trying to push everyone into physical existence. The opposing side felt God wasn't giving them any say in the matter. The two sides fought for what would be several thousands of our years. Michael had disarmed Lucifer when the dust settled, and Auriel had disarmed his son M*****.

Once the war was over, God told Lucifer and his followers that he would give them what they wanted. They would never be able to be reborn into physical form. They seemed happy with the decision, but God told them they could no longer live among the other white light souls. To that end, He created a rift into a dark dimension, and the fallen angels were forced into the rift to live in darkness for the rest of their existence. Over time they have grown bitter, angry, and vengeful. Eventually, they could figure out ways to enter our world, influence people, and ruin lives.

SPIRITUAL WARFARE

Most people don't believe spiritual warfare exists, and if they do believe in it, they don't see themselves as a part of it. They believe that angels and demons are fighting in another realm of existence, which has nothing to do with them.

Some people don't believe in either heaven or hell; they see it as a manmade concept to either make us feel better knowing we are going to a better place (i.e., heaven) or keep us on the straight and narrow with the threat of ending up in hell.

Still, others don't even think about it; they live for the moment and completely disregard what happens at the end of their physical existence.

I am here to tell you spiritual warfare is real, and I have been in the battle for over forty years. It's not your traditional battle, no guns, no bullets. It's basically hand-to-hand combat using weapons such as white light swords, spears, and hand grenades. The dark ones use swords, dark energy weapons made of fear, hate, and anger. As in any war, there are casualties, and the wounded abound. Two elite groups lead the army of light; the first is called the Legion of Light, and the second group is known as the Assassins. Michael, Auriel, Gabriel, Zebulim, and Raphael are the five archangels who make up the Legion of Light.

The Assassins are the archangels who guard the throne of God; they are made up of Auriel, Zyprhin, Dedria, Tomas, and Syphiam. The Assassins would equate to an elite sniper group, trained to kill with the least amount of fuss. When the war between heaven and hell was over, the Assassins were mothballed. After all, what do you do with trained killers but keep them close to you where you can keep an eye on them. So, you have them guard the throne of God.

The Legion of Light are the generals under the command of God and Jesus. Some of these warriors have volunteered to return to the physical world to help train people to fight the darkness on the physical plane of existence. They trained the other warriors, and they, in turn, trained the rest of the army.

It's a never-ending cycle, and we mortal beings are kind of at the mercy of both sides. My role in the war has always been that of a demon slayer. I have done God's work by removing demons and training lightworkers in all my lifetimes. I have personally been training people in what to look for, how to defend themselves, and how to help others plagued by negatives.

First, you help those being set upon by the negatives, once they are free, you have them help others, and if they cannot help the person themselves, they refer them to me. We lightworkers will continue to train the living and fight the negatives as best we can with our gifts.

Eight archangels have been born into the world today. I am one, and there are seven others which I have found and been in contact with seven of them. It is up to us to keep the balance and protect the living.

Not all archangels make the transition to the physical world unfazed. Some become mentally unstable because this transition does not go smoothly. Others get confused, thinking that they have multiple personality disorders or schizophrenia. When their soul consciousness is trying to merge with the physical consciousness, it can be very confusing and traumatic for the angel making the transition into the physical world.

The transition is not always easy; you may think you're going crazy, hearing voices in your head and thoughts that don't belong to you. Those who are lucky enough to make the transition with their soul and physical consciousness intact are left to find the others and help them understand what is happening to them. I have been able to help six of them, two in England, one in France and Italy, and another in America. One of the eight did not make the transition intact, and she suffered from severe mental illness. All of the archangels that are reborn have psychic and mediumistic abilities. Some come into their gifts as children, while others happen later in life.

It's never easy coming to terms with the fact that you have an Archangel inside of you, as I know myself. It can be difficult to accept that you have a separate consciousness inside of you. You must learn how to utilize and communicate with it. If you learn to make the connection, the soul consciousness can be a wealth of help and information. It can help you make decisions about the future and communicate with those on the other side, including your loved ones.

When you have your gifts from childhood on, you notice that your gifts evolve, change, and grow. Growing up without any support for your abilities makes it twice as hard for you to deal with everything. I was lucky enough to have my grandmother, a psychic medium, help me for the first five years of my life. She helped me to understand what I was seeing and hearing.

With my grandmother's death in 1979, my support in the physical world was gone. I could still connect with her on the other side, but it's not quite the same. Even though I had her to help me for the first five years, it's been a long road of discovery for me.

In 1988 I died and went to the other side, where I found out I had the soul of Auriel, the archangel existing inside of me. Ever since then, I have been in the thick of spiritual warfare, doing battle with demons. No one in their right mind would volunteer for this; it is a calling, one you cannot turn down.

LUCIFER

Lucifer, whose name means the shining one, is the most powerful of all the fallen angels. He is a self-appointed leader. Before the war, he was intelligent, ambitious, self-serving, logical, and determined to become the leader of the white light realm. Oh, he could be generous and patient with those closest to him, but he could be unforgiving and even cruel at times with others.

If you crossed him in any way, there were extreme consequences; he demands strict obedience from those who served him or those closest to him. If you had him as a friend, it was because you had earned his trust, which is difficult to do. If you are his friend, he will do everything in his power to protect and defend you should the need arise.

Before the war began, he had a handful of close friends, mostly archangels. His closest friend was Haniel, and even though Haniel sided with God, he respected his decision. Haniel is in physical form right now, and Lucifer stops by to visit him from time to time.

Lucifer must constantly be on his guard against his followers, as some would move against him if they had the chance. It has already happened to him once, and that demon and his followers paid for it with their life.

Lucifer supports most of the old demons, and he listens to their counsel on many things, but ultimately, he makes the final decision. He must deal with the lesser demons who are unruly at best and with rogue demons who want to do things their way. As in any Unitarian society, one must contend with unrest and deal with it with an iron hand, or anarchy will take over.

After being forced to reside in the dark realm, he had to come to terms with the fact that he would never rule the heavenly realm or see his closest friends on the opposing side again. Over the centuries, he and his followers have managed to find ingenious ways to infiltrate the physical world.

Here are a few ways they can create incursions into the physical world.

- Dark portals- doors that swing both ways- where they can come and go into our world at will.
- Humans create portals either by accident, i.e., paranormal investigations, Ouija board use, or on purpose, summoning negatives through black magic ceremonies.
- Incursions use a rip in the veils between the dark realm and the physical world to send dark energy through.

Lucifer tries to maintain control of his followers by assigning tough taskmasters to watch over and keep a tight rein on them. He has placed his closest associates in positions of power. He delegates a lot of discipline and policing to those he trusts the most. Over the centuries, there have been those who have plotted to take him down. He has always maintained control by using cunning, discernment, and strength. He makes sure to maintain an impenetrable façade for those around him. To show anything other than strength would be seen as a weakness and leave him vulnerable to attack.

He has a few close friends in the white light realm who he meets with from time to time to talk about the old times. He never discusses current issues with them but rather enjoys their company. These visits are kept strictly between him and his friends; no one else in the dark realm is aware of these.

He has absolute respect for the Legion of Light, God, and Jesus. He has the most regard for Auriel the Archangel and demon slayer. He knows if there is a job that needs doing, he can talk to her, and she will give him the truth no matter who is involved. He visits his friend Haniel periodically, who is in physical form. When Haniel asked him what he thought about Auriel, Lucifer replied, 'respect the assassin.'

The dark ones intend revenge against the white light souls who inhabit physical bodies. They want to make them pay for relegating them to the dark realm. And will stop at nothing to have their revenge on them.

HAUNTED OBJECTS

RELICS

I'm writing this chapter on haunted objects and relics because there is a lot of misinformation about them. It's not just a matter of locking these things away in a box or trunk; there's much more that needs to be done to make certain that these objects are kept away from people because of the harm they cause. People need information on how to deal with these things.

Haunted objects are not as prevalent as you would imagine. Only about 20% of the haunted objects encountered have negative entities attached to them. There's usually a reason for the attachment, such as a beloved doll or a favorite desk where writers spend most of their lives writing their books. In the case of haunted negative objects, someone may have bound the negative entity to the object. Such is the case of the Dybbuk box or Robert and Peggy, the haunted malicious dolls.

Most people believe that if the negative entity is bound to the object, it can't hurt you, but that's not true. Just because it is bound to the object does not mean its influence is bound solely to the object itself. Its influence can go far beyond the person who has the object. Its influence can and does reach out to others within the person's circle, acquaintances, and those who view the object.

If you visit a location where the doll is displayed, and you say something derogatory, and you leave. You get into a horrible car accident and almost die on the way home, not thinking about the object you just said negative comments about. When you stop to analyze the situation, it's only later that the truth dawns on you. The influence of the negative entity attached to the doll can reach out and cause all kinds of problems that may be harmful.

Most of the attachments to everyday objects are only human spirits who used or were attached to the object. Most of the time, they mean no harm; the object may have been cherished, and they are hard-pressed to separate themselves from it. They want to make sure that the object is preserved and loved with the same loving care they showed when they were alive. When it's a human spirit, it's a case of helping the spirit crossover into the light.

In the case of something like a Dybbuk box, a demon was called forth by two young Jewish girls during the Nazi occupation. They didn't realize what they had conjured up was a very old and powerful demon. They didn't know how to get rid of it, so they went to their grandmother, and she bound the demon to the box. It remained hidden for many years until a local man in Portland, Oregon, found the box at an estate sale. He bought it as a present for his mother. She immediately suffered a heart attack and almost died when she opened the box.

I recently received a call from a man who restores homes. He and his crew were pulling up floorboards in a house damaged by a fire. They pulled up a large section of boards, and hidden underneath the floor was a large book. They tried to pick up the book, but it was too heavy for one man to lift.

"I thought the guys were messing with me, so I tried to pick it up and couldn't do it by myself. It took two of us to lift it out of its hiding place. The book looked very old, and it was sealed with a wax seal. There was a name engraved in the wax." He told me.

He started to say the name, and I stopped him.

"Do not say the name; just spell it for me," I instructed him.

He spelled out the name Ast***th.

"That is a very old and very powerful demon's name. I knew there was a demon attached to the book; I could feel it. There is more than one bound to the book." Then an image appeared in my mind. "You opened the book, didn't you?" I said it was not a question but a statement of fact.

"Yeah, I opened it, and I know I shouldn't have." He said, "One of the workers took it home the first night, and he told me all manner of negative things happened at his house. It really scared him; he didn't want it in his house anymore."

"You should never have opened the seal on the book; now, something has to be done with it," I said, sighing heavily.

"What can I do with it? I found out that it was stolen from the Vatican long ago. When I was online trying to find out information on it, someone offered to buy it from me for thirty-two thousand. I don't like the way this thing feels." He said nervously.

"I can remove the demons attached to it, but you will have to seal it in a container with black salt and a crucifix," I warned him.

"I think I'll try to return it to the Vatican," He said.

"*Do not mail the book*; if it should get into the wrong hands, there is no telling what harm can be done. If I were you, I would call someone in the Vatican and let them know you have the book and want them to come and pick it up. They won't hesitate to send one of their exorcists to hand carry it back and place it in the vaults in the catacombs where it was stolen from." I impressed upon him the need to do this right away, no delay. "I will remove the demons attached to it right away, and you need to seal it in a solid dark container. Place holy water around the closure of the box and then put it inside a second container with more holy water and white salt, if you don't have any black salt."

"I'll do it right away; I want this thing gone!" He said vehemently.

"Make sure you do; these things can and will draw other demons to it!" I warned him.

GRIM REAPER

Everyone is fair game for the demons; no one is immune to their influence. It doesn't matter if you believe in them are not; they will make you a believer. The more faith you have, the bigger target you are. It seems to be a thing of pride for negative entities to victimize people of faith and clergy. They feel if they can turn someone of devout faith away from God and towards the darkness, then they have done their job.

The stronger the person's faith, the bigger the prize. The ultimate goal is to get people of faith to denounce God and all He stands for. It doesn't matter if you are a priest, rabbi, minister, chaplain's assistant, or devout Christian; it's all the same to them.

The more people of faith they can turn away from God, the happier they are. Even the lowliest person in the world, if they have great faith in God, can eventually overcome a demon simply by their unshakable faith. You must have faith in yourself, in God, in God's ability to defeat the demons. You must have faith that you can defeat just about anything Lucifer may throw at you.

The demon will try its best to wear you down to the point where you will do just about anything to get the demon away from you. It will try to brainwash you into thinking you will never be free of them or that they will kill you or those closest to you. They know you will do almost anything to protect yourself and those you love.

Sometimes you may find a demon waiting for someone to die. Most people don't understand that a demon will wait for an individual to die and collect their soul. They will enslave the soul and utilize it to get past lines of protection that have been laid down. If there is a holy line of protection laid down, nothing inhuman will be able to pass through the line. They will utilize a human spirit to move through the line and do their dirty work for them. They may have the human spirit cross the line to give the individual nightmares or attack them physically, emotionally, and mentally. It is not what the human soul wants to do, but it has no choice because the demon controls it.

Here is an actual event that occurred in 1981 when I was 20 years old and stationed at Fairchild Air Force Base as an EMT. It was the first time that I actively interacted with a demonic entity, even though I had been seeing and hearing them all my life.

I was working the night shift when I received a phone call from a company commander.

"Fairchild emergency specialist Collras here; what is the nature of the emergency?"

"This is Tech Sargent Wallingford over at the air refueling barracks. I have an airman that hasn't been seen for three days. Some men reported he attended a barrack party on Friday night and hasn't been seen since. Someone reported they saw him leave the party and go up to his room. He didn't show up for his Monday morning Chaplin duties, which is unlike him. He's very dedicated."

"Has anyone checked his room?" I asked.

"No one realized he was missing until this morning. I don't want to go in without medical backup just in case something is wrong." He said grimly.

"Alright, we'll be right there," I told him.

Hanging up, I went in search of Boggs, one of the other EMTs on duty with me. I found him in the breakroom enjoying a cup of coffee.

"Hey, we need to roll out. I just got a call from a Tech Sarge at the Air Refueling Company." I told him.

He stood up, pouring his coffee down the sink drain. "What's up? You look kind of off, and that's not normal for you," he commented.

"I have a bad feeling about this call," I responded.

He looked at me curiously, "What kind of bad feeling? The he's dead kind or you're otherworldly one?" he asked.

Boggs was one of the few people who knew about me being a psychic medium. His grandmother was a voodoo practitioner, and she took psychics and mediums seriously.

"Something doesn't feel right, so be careful and make sure you have your protective charm with you," I advised him.

"I started wearing it daily since you and I became ambulance partners. Since I've been working with you, all kinds of strange things have happened." He confided, grinning.

"Well, I did promise you it would never be boring working ambulance duty with me," I said, grinning back at him.

"You surely did; it's no wonder the others don't want to do ambulance duty with you!" He laughed.

"Hey, I just thought you liked working with the weird person," I said, laughing.

"I do, I spoke with my grandmother just before we started working together, and she gave me a bit of advice. 'You stick close to your partner, she's powerful, and she'll protect you.' I always listen to her because she's always been right." Boggs said, grinning from ear to car.

"Well enough, chit-chat, we need to get over to the barracks and see what's going on."

We gathered our equipment, got in the ambulance, and headed for the flight line area. Arriving at the barracks, Sargent Wallingford was waiting for us. We pulled out the stretcher and basic equipment and followed the Sargent to the second floor. Having no elevators in the building, we carried the gurney up the stairs to the second floor. Halfway down the corridor, we stopped in front of a room with the name Anderson on it.

"This is his room, I'll let you in, but I won't go in until you've accessed the situation." He informed us.

He's afraid of what he'll find if he goes in by himself. I thought. Using his master key, he unlocked and opened the door.

"What's his name?" I asked

"Airman Anderson." The Sargent responded.

"No, his first name," I said, feeling frustrated at the Sergeant's lack of compassion for the man in the room.

"Charles," I called his name softly.

Slowly pushing the door completely open, I saw a young man sitting on the floor with his legs pulled up and his head resting on his knees. There was what looked to be urine on the floor, and the room smelled of death. As I walked further into the room and got closer to him, I could see his chest was barely moving. I heard an odd growling sound coming from the left of me. Glancing over my left shoulder, I could see a black humanoid-like form standing in the corner. If there was such a thing as a Grim Reaper, this was it.

It startled me at first, then five years of medical training kicked in, and I focused on what I was there to do. I knew it was a demon, having seen them all my life. I knew from previous observations that this creature was waiting for the young man to die. But I was bound and determined it was not going to happen on my watch!

I completely ignored the entity and focused on the young man. Taking his vital signs, we assessed his level of consciousness. His blood pressure was abnormally low, his heart rate was erratic, and his breathing was labored and sketchy. He barely responded to any external stimuli and appeared almost comatose.

"Let's get him on the stretcher, then we can radio the ER and let them know what we have coming in," I ordered Boggs.

"Right, is it me, or do you feel something negative around here?" He responded grimly.

I gave him a pointed look, which told him not to ask any questions.

Emptying the gurney of our equipment, we picked the young man up and placed him on the gurney. It was hard going to get everything down the stairs to the entryway. We loaded the patient and equipment into the ambulance. I sat in the back with the patient monitoring his vital signs. It would be hard to get a line placed for the IV as he was dehydrated. I didn't see any signs of the negative entity during the ride to the hospital. I was hoping that would be the last I saw of it. Pulling up to the emergency entrance, we unloaded the patient and took him straight into the first exam room.

The ER DO (duty officer), Dr. Phipps, came into the room and examined the patient. He ordered labs, x-ray, IV, and oxygen and left the room, leaving me alone with the patient. I moved to the far side of the room to get the blood draw tray. As I turned back to the patient, I saw the demonic Grim Reaper standing by the side of the gurney. Its arms reached out for the young man.

I was so mad at the entity I fairly screamed at it telepathically: "You leave him alone he's not for you!"

It turned to look at me, and I could see its red glowing eyes staring at me full of hate and disdain.

"Stupid mortal, this one is mine; he belongs to me!" it screeched, growing larger. As it glided closer to me, I became conscious of a strong smell of sulfur which almost burned my nose. It turned away from me as if I were of little importance. It reached out its hands, and I could see them enter his body, struggling to pull the man's life force and soul from his body.

Suddenly I could hear a powerful voice telling it, "Stupid demon, do you think you can take what belongs to us?" I knew the voice was telepathic, and it was coming from me. "No, I think not! I command you in the name of God and Jesus Christ to leave now."

Whatever it was that the demon saw in my face seemed to startle it, and the next second it disappeared. I could feel the relief flood through my body, and I began to shake. Trying to stop my shaking, I busied myself starting an IV and drawing Charles's blood. Looking up after drawing the blood, I noticed his eyes were open, and he was staring at me in bewilderment.

"It's going to be okay, Charles, you rest. My name is June, and I'll be taking care of you." I reassured him.

He nodded his head, and for the first time, I noticed his breathing was normal. Taking his vital signs, I noticed his pulse was now steady, and his blood pressure was on the low side of normal.

"Dr. Phipps, the patient is conscious," I called out to the desk.

Dr. Phipps and Boggs came hurrying into the room. As the doctor did a quick examination on Charles's, he opened his eyes for a moment.

"I'm thirsty. Can I have some water?" He asked.

"Sure." Dr. Phipps told him. Turning to Boggs, he said. "Get him a small glass of water and make certain he only sips it." He instructed him.

"June, arrange for a bed in ICU. I want him monitored closely over the next forty-eight hours." He said, writing up the orders for his care.

I arranged for the bed and reported to the next shift. After our shift, Boggs and I left the building together. Once outside, Boggs asked, "So what was there? I could feel something, and it didn't feel good." He asked.

Reaching my car, I locked the door and turned to look at him. "It was a demon, and it was slowly killing him; by draining his life force."

"Jeez, I knew it felt negative. Damn, grandma's not going to believe this; see you Saturday." He said, heading for his car.

I called my grandmother Edith when I got back to my apartment.

"Hey, grandma, how are you feeling?"

"I'm fine, June Ann. What's up? You usually don't call me this early." Edith said.

I relayed the events of the day to her.

"Well, this was one demon you had to confront; it sounds like the creature was going to kill the young man if you hadn't intervened. You did the right thing." She confirmed. "How's the young man?"

"He seemed to be on the mend physically, but mentally it's a whole different thing. I'll check on him before I go on my next shift." I told her.

I had the next two days off and left early for my Saturday morning shift as I wanted to stop by and see Charles. When I arrived at his room, Dr. Rosembaum was just leaving. I spoke with the staff to find out how he was doing.

"Hello June, I hear you brought this guy in; you saved his life." He commented.

"Yeah, you could say that. How is he doing mentally? I just found out from the head nurse that someone slipped some PCP into his soda at the party. I sure would like to find the person who did it and do a little something for them. For God's sake, he's a Chaplin's assistant. I don't think he would hurt a fly." I told him.

"He'll heal physically, but this has taken a toll on him mentally and emotionally. I'm going to recommend a medical discharge; I think it will be best for him to go home and heal."

"I think you're right; he can heal better at home where he feels safe and secure."

"Well, have a nice visit; he's going to be discharged tomorrow, and They'll see him on an outpatient basis for a few weeks until they can get him as stable." He assured me and headed down to the nursing station to do his charting.

I knocked on Charles's door and heard a soft 'come in.' I found Charles sitting in a chair by the window, opening the door, looking outside.

"Hello Charles, I don't know if you remember me; I'm June; I'm one of the techs who brought you into the ER," I told him, smiling encouragingly.

"Thanks for helping me. I don't remember much after the party. I've had a nightmare about this black figure telling me it would take my soul. Then the dream changes, and a fierce-looking female archangel appears and sends the demon away." He said in bewilderment.

"I think it's God's way of letting you know that he will protect you against evil," I said, trying to put a positive spin on it.

He was quiet for a few minutes, "I think you're right; he would never desert me, and it's not everyone who gets visited by an archangel." He said thoughtfully.

We talked for several more minutes; then, I headed down to the ER to start my shift. I visited him every day while he was in the hospital, and he would drop by the ER for a visit when he was attending his therapy sessions. A month later, he left for home, and I never saw him again.

HEARING THE OTHER SIDE

Everyone hears, sees, senses, and interprets the other side differently. There are many facets to how I hear, see, and communicate with the other side. There are good and bad sides to doing what I do. The good side is I can still see and hear my loved ones like my grandmother and grandfather. The downside is that I have days when I must deal with negative entities.

The first recollection I have of hearing the other side was when I was around four. It sounded like I was in a room filled with people, and everybody was talking simultaneously. It was confusing and overwhelming for me. My grandmother noticed that I was holding my hands over my ears.

Once she ruled out a physical hearing problem, she knew it must be how or what I was hearing from the other side. But she didn't know if it was what I was hearing or if it was just too loud for me, so she sat me down to talk and find out. At first, she thought I might have an ear infection, so she took me to the doctor, but there was no infection.

"June Ann, what's wrong with your ears?" My grandmother Edith asked.

"Everyone's talking; everyone's talking. Make them stop!" I told her, holding my hands over my ears.

"OK, we can fix this. Does it sound like there is a lot of people in here talking at the same time? Or is it what they're saying?" Edith asked.

"Everyone talking at the same time, I can't understand what they want or what they're saying."

"Alright, close your eyes and listen to me. Find a voice that's louder than the others and concentrate on it. Do you hear the voice?" Edith asked.

After a moment or two, I was able to pick out one voice among all the others. "Yes, it's a lady."

"Ask the lady her name and who she is to you," Edith instructed me.

"She said her name is Ann, and she's my sister. Grandma, do I have a sister?"

"You had an older sister Ann who died three years before you were born. She must have been assigned to watch over you." My grandma surmised. "Is there anyone else you can hear?"

Closing my eyes, I listened again for another voice. Suddenly I could hear someone whispering in my ear. "Hello June Ann, my name is Hannah, and I'm your great-great-grandma; I am one of your guardian angels."

"She says her name is Hannah, and she's my great-great-grandmother."

"Yes, my grandmother's name was Hannah, so this must be her watching over you. It sounds like you have at least two angels watching over you." Edith told me.

"Is that good, grandma?"

"Yes, it's very good; I'm happy they're taking care of you." She said, hugging me. "Are you still hearing all the other voices?"

"Yes, I can still hear them, but they're not as loud."

"Good, just Listen to your two guardians, and the others will fade into the background. If they start to get loud again, just tell Ann or Hannah to make them be quiet."

"Okay"

It took practice, but eventually, I learned how to tune the others out and tune into the other souls around me when needed.

As a young child, I did not have an extensive vocabulary and understanding of the meaning behind the larger words. During this time in my life, angels and spirits would communicate using pictures and feelings. I could see the spiritual beings with my physical eyes, but the images were unclear. I saw them as a hazy outline.

As I transitioned from early childhood to six years of age, how I perceived angelic beings changed significantly. Instead of getting images, sporadic words, and feelings, I could have full conversations. My ability to 'see' spiritual beings clarified, and I started to see them as I saw the living.

In the beginning, I saw demons as blobs of darkness, which hurt my eyes to look at. As I reached the age of five, my perception of them changed to how I see them today. I see them in their true form. Normally people will see negative entities as they wish to be perceived. They will reach into your mind and pull out the image you have created of what a demon should look like. Then amplify the image to create an image that will invoke terror in the person. No two people will see these creatures exactly the same.

In their true form, demons stand around seven feet tall and have a wingspan of about twelve feet. They are onyx black, and for the most part, they have a humanoid appearance, except for their face. When I see their face, it is the reflection of everything evil. The face itself has few features except for the glowing red or yellow eyes. If people were to see negatives as I do, they would never be the same again. I have had three people who requested to see what I see. The first was a medium friend of mine, the second was Zak Bagans of Ghost Adventures show, and the third was an ordained minister friend. All three regretted their request and had nightmares for some time after seeing the negatives in their true form.

It was very confusing for me when my empathic abilities kicked in at around five years. An empath is a person who picks up on other people's or spirits' emotions. It was hard for me to distinguish whether I felt my feelings or someone else's. As I was living with my mother, it was doubly difficult for me. Other people's emotions tended to overwhelm me, and it was worse during school. My grandma Edith was a great help in teaching me how to tell the difference.

I would ride my bike to my grandma's house, and she would give me exercises to help me distinguish who was feeling what. She also helped me to learn to block out other people's feelings. It took me several months to learn to become proficient at it.

I soon learned to tune my mother and her negative emotions out. Living with her was hell; even after I learned to block her negativity, life was never easy. I also started to experience what people call the knowing. The knowing occurs when you instantly know information, but you don't know where the information is coming from.

My abilities evolved through my teen years, becoming stronger and more diversified. I found I could do psychometry look at a photo, email, or letter to connect with a person and see a person's past lives.

I hear angels, spirits, and ghosts as if I were talking to you. It took me a few years to learn how to hear them clearly. At first, I received impressions, feelings, and words that sometimes did not make sense. Around six years old, it evolved into full-on conversations, although with my limited vocabulary, I did not always understand all of the words.

THROUGH MY EYES

People have no concept of how I do the things I do. People to understand that everyone hears, sees, senses feels and interprets the other realms differently. There are many ways that individuals see different realms of existence. It's all about how the brain interprets what they see, influenced by their beliefs and knowledge. We all agree the white light realm is tremendously beautiful, and the dark side is the things of which nightmares are made. Ninety-nine percent of people would not be able to tolerate seeing a negative in its true form.

I have grown up seeing demons without a preconceived image. Just because I see negatives in their true form does not mean I like to look at them. Over time, you become desensitized to what you are seeing. At first, as a child, it scared me, but Archangel Michael taught me that it is inside of them that you should be the most afraid of and not their external image.

I do not remember how old I was when I first started seeing negative entities, or as some call them, demons. It seems like they have always been around. It's not like they are a rarity, quite the contrary. I see them quite frequently, but it is usually in passing. I remember seeing dark shapes, blobs, and masses at around four or five years old. It was overwhelming for me when at about 4 ½ or five years old, I was able to see the negatives in their true form.

What I see is a black angel who stands seven feet tall. Its wings drag the ground as they walk; I would estimate they have a wingspan of about twelve feet. They have a humanoid appearance and are blacker than the darkest night. Their face is devoid of features except for their eyes. When you look into what passes for a face, you see the reflection of everything evil that is or ever has been.

My grandmother was unsure of what I was seeing as she had only seen a couple of negative entities in her life, and both were black masses. She decided to call on Archangel Michael to help her figure out what I was seeing.

"Michael, I need your help." She said, closing her eyes and opening herself to the telepathic communication.

"JuneAnn is seeing negatives for the first time in their true form and is scaring her. I will help her understand why she is seeing them in this manner. I will teach you, too, so you will understand what she is seeing."

I was coloring at the dining room table when Michael came to me.

"JuneAnn, you will no longer see the dark ones as a mortal but see them through angelic eyes. You used to see them as blobs of black, but now that you're older and your brain can comprehend their true form, you will always see them like this." He said gently.

"But why do they look like black angels? Except for their face, their face is hideous, and it hurts my eyes to look at them." I told him.

"You have to understand they were once angels and were made of pure white light energy. However, they were sent into the darkness when they turned their back on God. Living in the darkness and being so filled with hate, anger, jealousy, and revenge, they have become the darkness." Michael replied quietly.

He knew I needed time to process what he had just said, so he sat quietly with me at the table. Several minutes went by before I spoke.

"Do other people see them as I do? Can grandma see them like that too?" I asked him seriously.

"No, only you can see them in this way. Your grandmother sees and feels them differently." Michael said.

"Why do I see them in this way? Why am I different?" I asked him curiously.

"You don't know it yet, but you are special; even your grandmother doesn't know just how special you are. She will learn later, and so will you. It's a good special; you are the only one like you in the world today."

"I guess it's okay if I have to see them like this; I suppose I'll get used to it," I said, resigning myself to the fact that I would always see them this way.

My grandmother, who had been listening in the doorway, wondered about just how special I was. She had asked Michael before, and he had responded to say it was not for her to know right now. "She is old beyond her years, Michael, and that is what worries me. I will not be here forever to help her."

"She can hear the negatives, understand their language, and see them in their true form. They cannot hide what they are from her; she will see through any illusion they throw at her. She needed to see them in their true form, so when she gets older, she will be able to do battle with them." Michael told her.

"It's true then; she is the one the family prophecy foresaw coming. If she is, she is exceptional." Edith surmised.

"It is all that I can tell you, and you must not tell the child or anyone else," Michael warned her.

"I won't; who would believe me anyway?" She responded wryly.

Before this time, I could see the spiritual beings with my physical eyes, but the images were unclear. I started to see them as I saw people. I saw them as a hazy outline — my ability to 'see' spiritual beings clarified as I grew older.

I still see the negative entities in their true form today. If people were to see negatives as I do, they would never forget what they saw or how they felt

HELP FROM ABOVE
(1198 ad)

We are living in a time of great spiritual warfare; God (the greater consciousness) has heard humanity's cries for help. He has sent archangels (warriors of light) back to live physical lives to find, remove and, in some cases, destroy the creatures of darkness. He has sent warrior angels in angelic form into the world to walk among the living. These reborn archangels retain their powers even while in physical form. Once such warrior of light is Auriel, she is a demon slayer and defender of heaven. When the living asks God for help, He does answer, maybe not in the way we would like or expect.

Over the last seventy years, warrior angels have been reborn into physical bodies. They teach the living how to defend and protect themselves against the invading darkness. Their sole job is to bring awareness of these negatives and spread the word to the living.

Sometimes we, as humans, become lost in our daily lives or in the quest for fame, power, and wealth. It is then that some turn to dark beings to help them achieve their goal instead of working for it. They used to call it making a pact with the devil. We, as humans, always seem to want the quick fix. We seek divine intervention to get us out of trouble when it all goes wrong. People think there will be no repercussions for what they have done, but it all comes down to you reaping what you sew. Here is the true story of a woman who made a deal with a dark being, and when it turned on her, she asked God for help.

1198 AD

Some people seek to summon a negative entity (demon) to do their bidding. The person believes they can control the demon once they summon it. However, what happens is, at first, the demon will comply with the person's demands. Once the negative entity has lulled them into a false sense of security, they will turn on the person and take possession of them, making their life a living hell.

The person is completely under their control. If the person is strong enough, they will seek help for their attachment. Prayer is a strong weapon against the darkness, and God does hear your prayers for help when this happens. Sometimes he answers your prayers in a way you least expect it. Here is a real story, as shown to me by archangel Michael.

The year was 1198 AD, Sussex, England. A woman in her early twenties is crying out for help in desperation. She is lying on the thatched floor, covered in dirt. Her dress was ragged and tattered; her feet were bare and callused. Her face is covered in dirt; the only clean area is where the tears running down her cheeks have washed the dirt away.

"Help me, dear God, help me, take this evil from me." The woman cried out in anguish, rising to her knees, she sobbed in despair. Her once blonde hair, matted and brown with dirt, hung nearly to her waist. It fell around her tear-stained face as she sobbed.

Suddenly a bright light filled the dingy room; as she looked towards the source of the light, she saw a huge female angel with long dark auburn hair and blue-green eyes staring down at her. The look on her face was one of disdain.

"Foolish mortal, you play at things which are best left alone, and then you seek divine intervention! I have been called upon to remove the demon from you." The angelic being informed her impatiently.

"Who is it that has answered my prayer?" The woman asked.

"God, the father, has heard your prayer and sent me, Auriel archangel and demon slayer, to help you," Auriel responded.

The woman's face changed dramatically, and the archangel observed the demon come to the surface. The woman's eyes turned black, her voice became guttural, and her countenance was one of pure evil.

"Who are you to challenge me? This mortal summoned me of her own free will; she is mine." The entity growled, speaking in Aramaic with an evil smile. "If you try to remove me, I will kill her."

Auriel grinned at the demon, "Stupid creature; if you knew me, you would know that I do not care if she lives or dies."

Giving no thought to what would happen to the woman, Auriel reached inside her body and ripped the demon from her. At that moment, the woman's body died, and her soul was released.

Holding the demon by the throat, Auriel examined its face looking to see if it was one she had dealt with before. "I see we have met before, S******; you should have learned your lesson the first time."

"I'm not afraid of you!" the dark entity growled, spewing foul language and insults at her.

But the look in its eyes told her a different story; it was a look of pure fear. "You're lying as usual; I can see the fear in your eyes. You must be a particularly stupid demon." She said disdainfully.

The comment made the demon even angrier. "You will answer for this. I know God cherishes His precious humans, so you will have Him to contend with!" it snarled, renewing its efforts to break free from her hold.

"It will be worth it to send you back where you belong. Maybe I should just kill you now!" She shook the demon roughly and decided she'd had enough of it. Creating a white light infinity orb (a sphere of pure white light energy which can imprison the negative entity), she dropped the demon into the orb and cast the orb down towards the darkness. When the orb reached the edge of the dark realm, it dissolved, dumping the entity back where it belonged.

"Auriel," she heard God calling for her.

Michael appeared next to her, "He's upset with you; you know it's against his wishes to cause harm to the humans." He reminded her sternly.

"It's the human's fault; she should never have summoned it!" she argued.

"I agree she did summon it, but that's not the point, and that's not how He will see it." He warned her.

Auriel appeared before God (the Greater consciousness) and bowed. "You sent for me, Father."

"You know I value your work and the good you do, but this was your last offense. You seem to have no compassion, care, or love for the human race." He said censure in his voice.

"From what I have seen of them, they have no reverence for the life you give them. They take from the earth and the animals without thought. They prey on each other, filled with greed, jealousy, and dissension." Auriel said.

"Have you forgotten that you were once like them, a primitive race filled with petty emotions? You came to see the error of your ways, but it took you several millennia to do it. You have been too long in our world and have forgotten how to have compassion for humankind. You have grown hard and uncaring."

"I have seen what humans do with the gift of life you have given them. Your gift is wasted on them. The soul which resides within the physical vessel learns little from experience. I have watched them for centuries; they abuse the land, animals, water, and each other. Their curiosity, sense of entitlement, and the quest for power lead to nothing but chaos." She responded with conviction.

"I agree they have much to learn and little patience to learn it. The thought has crossed my mind from time to time. Do you think I don't get upset with men, don't want to erase them and start anew?

It's then I remember how eventually chaos gave way to order, and with the order came enlightenment." He reminded her patiently.

"But Father, they summon the dark ones, harm each other. None of these actions are worthy of the souls that inhabit the body." She insisted.

"I knew there would be problems, which is why I created the Avenging and Warrior Archangel Divisions. They dispense justice to the living. You are one such archangel; you have the ability and the knack for dispensing justice and retribution when and where it is needed." He said with pride in his voice.

"If it were up to me, I would wipe out around 70 percent of humankind. I think it was a very bad idea to give humans free will." She stated vehemently.

"I know your opinion on man, and in some ways, I agree, but I have already punished them once, and I have promised not to do it again."

"But..."

"Enough child, I have made my decision regarding the death of the woman. You will go back and live physical lives until you have learned to have compassion and understanding for humanity. It may take you many lifetimes to come to terms with it, but you must experience this for yourself to grow and understand." He pronounced judgment.

"Noooo," She implored, "Anything but that!"

Michael appeared beside her.

"I have made my decision. Michael, you will oversee her lives." He announced, turning he walked away.

"Yes, Father." He agreed, watching Him disappear.

"You know it could have been worse; you could have had Raphael instead of me," Michael said, trying to make light of the situation.

"This is the worst thing I can ever imagine happening. To live among humans in a physical shell, I don't know if I can bear it." She told him, her voice filled with despair.

In all the millennia, Michael had been with Auriel; he had never seen her this way. He grew concerned at her lack of fight. He knew he had to do something to help her.

"Listen to me, Auriel; I will always be with you in all of the lives you live in the physical world. I will never be far from your side. I know this is going to be hard for you to bear, but you need to see the bright side of being stuck in a physical body." Michael reassured her.

"What good can possibly come from being confined to a prison of flesh?" she asked him forlornly.

"You will be able to do demonic removals when you are in the physical body. The negatives won't be able to detect your presence. They will think the body is all there is, and they will never suspect you are hiding inside. Then you can come forward and remove them from the physical world. It will be like the old days when we had to hunt them down." Michael said, grinning at her.

She thought about it for a moment or two, and he could see her weighing in all the possibilities. "Maybe it won't be so bad after all." She said. "Another good point is humans don't have very long lives, so I'll be back here fairly quickly." She reasoned.

Michael knew she had forgotten how slowly time passed in the physical world versus the angelic realm. He decided it was wiser not to bring it up at that moment. It was bad enough she had to be confined to a physical form. If she realized how slow the time would pass, it would only anger her. It was not the time or place to remind her of the time difference when she was about to enter her first physical life in over ten million years. She would probably be upset with him later for not reminding her.

"When is the first life?" she asked him.

"We only have a moment or two." He responded.

"You won't leave me, will you? I'll always be able to hear you, won't I?"

"Yes, I will see to it that you can hear me, and you will also know who you are at some point in each lifetime. You will do the job you are most suited for, demon slayer. And you shall serve Him." Michael smiled at her.

"Thank you for being here for me; I don't think I would be able to endure it if you were not with me," she told him.

"I am your soul mate; I would never let you go through this without me by your side." He told her solemnly. He knew it was hard for her to admit she was afraid, so he said nothing.

CURSES

What is a curse, and are there different types of curses? The dictionary defines a curse as follows: **An evil prayer**: a malevolent appeal to a supernatural being for harm to come to somebody or something, or the harm that is thought to result from this

A curse, in reality, is either a human spirit that is earthbound seeking revenge by causing a chain of events or a demonic entity that has become attached to a person, place, or object.

Are curses real, or are they all in the person's mind? Curses are real, both in the person's mind and in paranormal circumstances.

Do curses travel through time? Curses can seem to travel through time because, as we know, there is no concept of time for demons and earthbound spirits. Here is an example of how a 'curse' can be set in motion.

The first is by a tragic event such as a death caused by either murder or what the person perceives as murder. What I mean by death due to a perceived murder is a death due to neglect or death that could have been prevented but was not. An example of this could be a mother that died in childbirth because the doctor would not tend to her.

This may be because she was of the wrong race social status or did not have the financial means to pay the doctor.

The mother's spirit would then haunt the doctor or his family for the wrong that was done to her or, if her child died, the child. The spirit can cause poltergeist-like activity, such as the movement of objects, being pushed, slapped, or scratched. They can cause harm or even death to people by pushing someone down the stairs, spooking a horse while a person is riding, or even starting a fire.

The mother's spirit would remain earthbound and continue to avenge the perceived wrong until either one of two things happen. The first is that it obtained revenge, or secondly, someone helped it see the error of its ways and cross completely over. This tragic event is sometimes all it takes to set a 'curse' in motion. This gives the impression that the family is cursed when in actuality, they are haunted.

People need to understand the reason behind the haunting or curse to lay it to rest. If you think your family is cursed, you need to do some digging to find out when the 'curse' began and what event triggered it. Hate, like love, is one of the strongest emotions known to man. Both of these intense emotions can and do transcend time and even death.

Here is an example of an object that people have said is cursed. The famous Hope diamond is said to be cursed as all of the owners of the jewel have either died a gruesome death or their life has been devastated after purchasing the diamond. People fail to understand that the so-called curse attached to this jewel is not a curse but a demon attached to the diamond. The first owner of the diamond used the jewel in satanic rituals. He used it to open a doorway to the dark side for his own selfish need for power and wealth. Using the jewel as an offering allowed a demon to become attached to it; therein lies the beginning of the 'curse of the Hope diamond.' When you make a deal with the devil, you always lose in the end.

An example of a place believed to be cursed is the burial chamber of King Tutankhamen. Some will tell you that the happenings were just coincidence; in my experience, there is no such thing as coincidence.

In the construction and sealing of the tomb, many workers died or were killed. It is a little-known fact that a human sacrifice was made to protect the tomb with the sealing of his tomb. The guard's blood was placed at the tomb entrance to protect it from grave robbers and to seal in the secret of the young king's death.

Even in death, the guard was devoted to the young king, having sworn an oath before he died to guard the tomb in this world and the next. The guard's spirit still roams the tomb of the boy king. He is unaware of the passage of time or that his services are no longer needed.

HOW TO HELP YOURSELF

AND

WHERE TO FIND HELP

The first thing you have to do is identify whether or not you have a negative entity problem. To do this, you need to determine whether the entity you have in your location is an inhuman or an earthbound spirit. Here are the perimeters to identify an inhuman spirit:

- A feeling of absolute dread.
- The atmosphere feels heavy and thick.
- You feel cold internally, which has nothing to do with the external temperature.

Once you have established that you have a negative entity problem, you will need help. The next thing you will have to do is determine whether the negative entity is attached to the home, land, or person. It would be best if you asked yourself a few questions:

1. When did the paranormal activity start?

2. Did you just move into the home or start doing renovations?

3. Is there a paranormal activity when the home is empty?

4. Are other people experiencing any paranormal activity if you are away from home? Or is it just when a single person is at home?

5. Is there any paranormal activity in other buildings on the land?

6. Are there certain rooms that feel different or that your animals will not go into?

Answering these questions will help you narrow down if there is an attachment to an individual, building, or a piece of land.   Once you find this out, you can move forward.

If it is a person to who the negative entity is attached, you must go straight to finding a local clergy. If it is the land or a building, you can contact a local paranormal group and have them do an investigation.

Here are a few things that have been known to calm down the activity temporarily:

- Tobacco under your pillow at night
- Saging the area (if the entity is negative, it will ramp up activity); after you sage, you will need

to seal the building using holy water and anointing oil (see below)
- Recordings of Buddhist chanting, religious sermons, religious music
- Lighting white candles certain Tibetan singing bowls if the frequency is right
- Pleading the Blood of Christ and God and Jesus (or use whatever deities name you believe in) name; *Father, in the name of Jesus, I now plead the Blood of Jesus to remove the demon which is attacking me. I now Plead the Blood of Jesus against demon attacking me. Father, in the name of Jesus, I have full faith and belief that the Blood of Jesus will protect me against any of the things that I have just Pled His Blood on. Thank you, Father. Thank you, Jesus."*
- You can also say: *In the name of Jesus Christ and God almighty, I rebuke thee Satan and all those who dwell in darkness*
- Holy water and the anointing oil- use the oil to make a sign of the cross above each door and window. Asking: In the name of God and Jesus Christ, I ask that nothing negative be allowed to enter this building. Let this oil protect us from negative intrusion.
- Bells- the ringing of a brass bell helps to ward off negative entities. This has to do with the harmonic vibrational frequency of the bell.

    A few paranormal groups have someone they can call to remove the negative entity. If the group you choose doesn't have someone, they may know of someone who might be willing to help.

A word of warning, just because a paranormal group comes out does not mean that they will find anything. The entity may be there, but sometimes they will sit back and watch what the humans are doing. They will observe the people involved with the paranormal group and see if they can sense their presence. If the investigators are getting no response, they may try to provoke the entity, which can be very dangerous. If it is a negative entity, it will react violently to the use of their names and prayers. The easiest way to find out if the entity is negative is to start saying prayers and invoking the name of God and Jesus Christ.

Once the paranormal group has investigated, they will review their findings with you. If they find the presence of a negative entity, they may try to do a house blessing or clearance. If the activity stops, it may have been a negative human spirit. If the activity gets worse, you will know for certain that it is not a human spirit but a demonic presence.

When you know for certain that this is an inhuman negative entity, you will need to seek help. One of the first places to start is with the clergy in your church. If you do not have a church you go to, seek out local clergy and ask them for guidance; let them know that you've had investigators come out, and they have identified it as an inhuman spirit. Most clergies have some training in house clearance, blessings, and exorcisms. They will assess the situation to determine whether they need to do an exorcism on the individual or the house and land.

If you cannot find clergy that will help, you must reach out to a deliverance minister, exorcist, or someone with my abilities.

If you choose to contact The Catholic Church, it may be a while before you get any help. Since 2018 they have been overwhelmed with verified cases of possessions. You must also go through several steps before they even send someone out to see you. It is a long and tedious process, but it will be well worth it if you are lucky enough for them to come out. Deliverance ministers are also a rarity. I only know three I have found reputable, and I have put their information at the end of this chapter.

I would advise you to steer clear of dark magicians, voodoo, and Santa Maria practitioners, as well as Brujas. Basically, anyone who summons spirits.

Two clergies I am acquainted with are Father Bob Bailey Bishop James Long. Deliverance ministers Keith and Carl Johnson and demonologist Farah Deel and Adam Blai.

Archbishop James Long:

www.facebook.com/bishopjameslong

Fr Robert Bailey:

www.facebook.com/frbob444

Adam Blai

http://www.religiousdemonology.com/

Keith and Carl Johnson:

www.facebook.com/DuoDaemonologie/

www.facebook.com/PanoramaParanormal/

demonologyinc.wixsite.com/home?fbclid=IwAR2h29xxGufC5u5pjfTGtEggG-IxJP-urJDHd1XeU9a7sxAurLPO3xZRhkc

Farah Deel:

www.paranormalsocieties.com/view_society.cfm?id=17660

GLOSSARY OF COMMON TERMS

Ascend – the soul enters the heavenly realm.

Angel- a white light entity made of pure positive energy. They are some of the oldest souls.

Archangel- An angelic being of great power, the oldest of the angelic beings who have dedicated its life to the service and defense of heaven. They are commanders who answer only to God.

Common Souls- these are the white light souls who most commonly reincarnate time and again to experience lives so they can to grow and evolve.

Cross over -when the soul of a person or animal transitions into pure complex heavenly energy.

Dark Ones- Inhuman entities such as: minions, demons, ugly, shadow person, creepy-crawly, succubus, incubus.

Earthbound- a person's soul which remains on the earthly plane of existence for a reason of its own.

Entity- A being made up of pure energy, whether good or bad.

Ghost-the soul of a person who remains in the earthly plane of existence.

Greater consciousness- A being or beings of pure light and energy, which is a constant presence in the universe. All souls are linked with the greater consciousness, which gives guidance, courage, and love to all souls.

Guardian- angelic beings are assigned to an individual to guide the living and offer help and support.

Infinity orb- a sphere of pure white light energy that can imprison the negative entity and protect a human, animal, or location.

Light beings- A white light entity that works for the greater good of all humanity.

Realm- A plane of existence separated from other dimensions by subtle vibrational frequencies.

Shadow person- an inhuman negative entity that has a humanoid form with red or yellow glowing eyes. It sometimes is described as wearing a hat.

Spirit- the soul when it has moved on from the earthly plane of existence.

White light- A pure energy source that can transcend time, space, and the physical world. A place of singular peace, love, and harmony which can heal physical beings.

Warrior angel- An angelic being trained by the archangels to defend heaven and humans against the dark entities.

Watchers- are neither all good nor bad; they are more impartial observers. On occasion, they can swing either way due to circumstances.

TO CONNECT WITH THE AUTHOR GO TO:
www.mysticconnections.org
https://www.facebook.com/june.lundgren
https://www.facebook.com/demonSeer
https://twitter.com/June91c

Other Author Books Available On:
Amazon.com

www.ingramcontent.com/pod-product-compliance
Lightning Source LLC
Chambersburg PA
CBHW051429290426
44109CB00016B/1490